37-8

152

Political Integration and Disintegration in the British Isles

Political Integration and Disintegration in the British Isles

A. H. BIRCH

London
GEORGE ALLEN & UNWIN
Boston   Sydney

Printed in Great Britain
in 10 on 11 point Times

Acknowledgements

My first thanks must go to the politicians and political organisers who have generously given me their time and contributed to my education. Without exception, they have been most helpful.

Secondly, I am grateful to the Nuffield Foundation for a grant of £300 which enabled me to start the research on which the book is based, and to the University of Exeter for contributing towards my travelling expenses.

I should also like to thank academic colleagues and friends who have given advice or exchanged ideas on some of the questions discussed in the book. They include Basil Chubb and Martin O'Donogue in Dublin, Alan Milne and Cornelius O'Leary in Belfast, James Kellas and Richard Rose in Glasgow, Henry Drucker in Edinburgh, Peter Madgwick in Aberystwyth, and Richard Clutterbuck, Bob Dowse, Jeffrey Stanyer and David Steel in Exeter. They bear no responsibility for what I have written, however, which they may or may not like when they see it.

My wife Dorothy has been of immense assistance in the later stages of writing the book, which increases still further my gratitude for her support and help over the years.

Exeter, January 1977   A.H.B.

Contents

List of Tables

1
Introduction

From 1922 until at least 1967 it was generally assumed that the United Kingdom was not only united but integrated – a national society affected by class divisions but not by the regional, ethnic or cultural conflicts that scarred political life in less fortunate countries. In the last few years this belief has suffered a series of shocks, most obviously in Northern Ireland but also by the growth of nationalist parties in Wales and Scotland demanding independence for their countries. There are now seven parties in the Westminster Parliament, after more than a generation in which there have been only three – the four new ones being nationalist rather than ideological in their orientation. A Royal Commission on the Constitution has recommended various forms of governmental decentralisation and both main parties – as well as all the minor ones – seem committed to institutional change.

In the welter of controversy which these disintegrative developments have created, there is a pressing need for a dispassionate examination of the reasons for their emergence and the problems they pose for our society. Our political leaders, while grappling with desperate economic problems, are also having to take far-reaching decisions about the future structure of British government. What powers should be given to the proposed national assemblies in Wales and Scotland? If they are to have legislative powers, should they also have the power and responsibility of levying taxation? If not, can it be expected that English taxpayers will subsidise policies over which their elected representatives have no control? Should Welsh and Scottish representation in the UK Parliament be reduced (following the example of Northern Ireland), and if so by what formula? Is it envisaged that the new assemblies could become constituent assemblies, if a majority of their members opt for secession? If not, how are they to be stopped from asserting this right? Should the English regions also be given greater control over their government, and if so by what means? Should regional economic policies be changed in the light of these developments, and if so how? This book cannot answer all these questions, but I hope that it may contribute to a more informed debate about them.

These recent developments in Britain and Ireland also raise questions of a more general and academic nature. For over a century, social scientists have been predicting that social and technological developments in industrial societies would lead to a gradual decline in traditional conflicts and particularistic loyalties. Their approaches and value-orientations have of course varied widely, but a common feature of many of their arguments has been the assumption that social progress would be accompanied by a diminution in the political significance of ethnic, religious and cultural divisions.

Thus, Marx and Engels believed that class conflict would become not only more severe but also more universal, so that the international struggle between workers and capitalists would relegate national, cultural and religious divisions to the side-lines of history. At the same time, sociologists have asserted that the growth of a mobile, functional society involves the replacement of traditional and local loyalties by a shared sense of values and the acceptance of political authority based on a bureaucratic and rational system of administration.

More recently, an influential school of political scientists, led by Karl Deutsch, have developed a model of nation-building in which the extent of social interaction and communication between citizens, as measured by various statistical indicators, is regarded as a clear guide to the extent of social and political integration. This last theory is the intellectual progenitor of the functionalist view of supranational integration which underlies the planning of the European Economic Community, based as it is on the belief that the best hope of replacing national loyalties by European loyalties is not by propaganda or dramatic constitutional changes but simply by developing the habit of co-operation through various functional institutions, accompanied by the growth of personal interaction and mobility.

These theories have always had their critics, but recent developments in many parts of the world suggest that the theories may be not only an imperfect guide to reality but in some respects seriously misleading. Although church attendance has declined in most industrial societies, in the Western democracies as a whole the correlation between religious affiliation and voting is still closer than that between class and voting. Linguistic divisions cause political conflict not only in under-developed countries like India but also in highly developed ones like Canada, Belgium and Wales. Racial conflicts grow sharper and more violent, not least in countries like the USA where racial minorities have recently made rapid progress in terms of civil rights. The EEC shows no obvious sign of replacing national loyalties by European loyalties. Far from ethnicity declining as a source of political passions, it seems to be growing in strength.

The final steps in political disintegration are secession or civil war. In the United Kingdom we now have a real threat of civil war in Northern Ireland together with two lively separatist movements on the mainland. We are not alone in this. In centralised France, the 'one and indivisible Republic', there are now separatist movements among the Bretons, the Basques and the Corsicans, all of them willing to engage in direct action, occasionally violent, to advance their cause. Even authoritarian regimes suffer the same problems, as is evidenced by the inability of the Spanish authorities to suppress the Basque nationalist movement and the intermittent rumblings that emerge from the Ukraine and Georgia.

We therefore face a paradox. In a world which is more interdependent than ever before, with instant communications, an explosion of international travel, and a multitude of international agencies, we seem to be experiencing a resurgence of local loyalties. What are the reasons for this? Does it look like a passing phenomenon or are its causes deeply rooted? Is the authority of the nation-state, so often said to be threatened by the development of supranational institutions and multinational companies, actually in greater danger from the dissension of internal minorities? These are important questions for all social scientists and they can only be analysed by re-examining the role of economic, political and cultural factors in national integration and disintegration. It is hoped that this study, while focusing on the British Isles, may throw some light on these large and general questions.

Approaches to the Problem

Political integration and disintegration are both historical processes and can only be understood in historical perspective. To appreciate the character and extent of integration in the United Kingdom it is essential to look again, albeit briefly, at the way in which the national state was built and consolidated. Since the UK included the southern counties of Ireland from 1801 until 1921, when what is now the Republic achieved its independence by armed conflict, the story includes not only a process of partial integration, pursued over several centuries, but also an outstanding example of disintegration. The Irish dimension is important in its own right, important for the continuing impact on British politics of the tragic conflict in Northern Ireland, and interesting for the fact that the normally peaceful British Isles harbour the world's most durable underground army, now over 60 years old and still in business with training camps, courts martial, and a variety of modern weapons. The fortunes of the Irish Republic may also be thought to offer clues as to what might happen if Wales or Scotland were to break away from England.

There is, however, no intention to pursue the issues chronologically, except in Chapter 2. We are concerned with a number of general issues and problems that have to be given analytical treatment. One of these is the economic effects of integration on the peripheral areas of the country. It is sometimes said that 'every country has its South' (a reference to Italy, not America), but the reasons for this deserve explanation, as do the overall consequences of different regional policies pursued by governments. Two other questions, important in many parts of the world, are the political effects of religious differences and the problems of maintaining a minority language, whose survival is bound up with a particular culture and way of life, in a world dominated by mass communications.

Another general question concerns the character and bases of national or sub-national loyalties, as held by both minority and majority groups within a state. The British Isles provide fascinating examples of such loyalties, but there is no single method by which they can be analysed. Public opinion polls provide very little evidence, since the number of non-English respondents in a national sample is normally too small to yield useful data. It is necessary to draw on a variety of sources and clues, including political behaviour, literature and the mass media. I have taken particular care to include a fair number of quotations to illustrate the emotions that are involved in the conflicts under discussion. Recent tendencies in the social sciences have made some academic work rather arid, and a well-known American scholar has complained that 'the prevailing modes of explanation do not enable political scientists to comprehend phenomena as fully as the forms used by some novelists, journalists, poets and film directors' (Kariel, p. 1089). Nationalist movements cannot be understood without some comprehension of the passions they arouse, and for this reason I shall quote not only from speeches and pamphlets but also from poems and folk-songs that express the feelings of the participants.

Since feelings are involved, I must admit that I am myself English and what I write will inevitably reflect a certain Englishness of outlook and experience. I apologise in advance for the possibility that some of my comments may irritate Irish, Scottish or Welsh readers and I hope they will note that my comments about English attitudes and policies are equally outspoken.

A brief word of explanation is also due to my fellow-academics. I had originally intended to write a book that was almost twice as long. I changed my mind about this because the rapid developments in relations between the constituent parts of the United Kingdom led me to think that a fairly short book, produced quickly and at a reasonable price, might help to inform the general public as well as academic students of politics and to contribute one or two ideas to the vitally important debates about the future of our country that are now taking place. I have therefore used only a part of the research material I collected, I have reduced the number of statistical tables, and I have thrown away my card index of potential footnotes. However, I have retained essential bibliographic references and I believe that the analysis will be found to illuminate the theoretical study of the processes of political integration and disintegration as well as the problems of my own country.

2

The Growth of the United Kingdom

Historical Outline

It is necessary to set the scene by establishing some basic facts about the growth of the United Kingdom as a political entity, which can be summarised quite briefly. England itself was brought under unified political control in the ninth and tenth centuries by the kings of Wessex, who extended their authority in stages from the area south of the Thames to the border with Scotland. In 1066 the kingdom was conquered by the Normans, who quickly took steps to consolidate their authority. A national tax, the Danegeld, had been collected before the Normans arrived, but the national register of property known as the Domesday Book, completed between 1068 and 1071, is a very early example of administrative penetration and control by a central government. The boundaries of England have been unchanged and unchallenged since that time, although for some centuries there were areas around the borders with Wales and Scotland in which the local lords maintained a large degree of independence from the king.

Wales and Ireland were invaded and partially conquered by Anglo-Norman lords in the twelfth and thirteenth centuries. The greater part of Wales was mountainous and not greatly coveted, but English castles were built at various points around the Welsh coast and there was some English settlement in the extreme south-west. Wales also served as a staging post to the more fertile lowlands of central Ireland. Neither of these countries had had a unified government of its own before the invaders arrived, power in Wales being in the hands of local chieftains and power in Ireland being divided between local landowners and the provincial governors or kings who exercised a tenuous kind of authority over their respective areas.

The first non-English territory to be politically integrated with England was Wales. From the twelfth century until the beginning of the nineteenth century, Ireland was treated in the manner of an overseas colony, in ways and with consequences that will be outlined below. But Wales was in an anomalous position. By the end of the Middle Ages the whole country had come under the loose control of English lords and the English king, who had acquired six counties (about half the country) in his personal capacity as landowner and feudal lord. But it was not subject to parliamentary laws, its citizens did not have the rights and duties of English subjects, and large areas of the country were in a somewhat anarchic condition. There was little effective control of smuggling and raids across the border with England.

In the reign of Henry VIII the Reformation brought Wales to the attention of the king and his ministers, for two reasons. First, it was thought that the country was a security risk, with its coastline open to invasion by the king's Catholic enemies and its people's loyalty open to question. Secondly, the 1534 Act of Supremacy, which made the king the head of the Church of England, created an anomalous situation in Wales, for that country was under the ecclesiastical jurisdiction of the Archbishop of Canterbury but was not under the legal jurisdiction of king and Parliament. For the dissolution of the monasteries and similar reforms to have legal effect in Wales it was necessary for Acts of Parliament to be applicable there, and considerations of this kind were the main immediate reason for the decision to extend Parliament's authority over Wales by the Act of Union of 1536 (see Rees, pp. 18–21).

This Act abolished the political powers of the Lords and divided Wales into twelve counties, to be governed in exactly the same way as English counties. In practice this meant that legislation and taxation were in the hands of Parliament while local administration and the maintenance of order were entrusted to the county magistrates. In the Welsh counties (as elsewhere) these were the local gentry, who were for the most part Welshmen who had become Anglicised. All official business was henceforth transacted in English, which was becoming the normal language of discourse among the landowning and educated classes. From 1536 onwards Wales had no governmental institutions that differed significantly from those of England until as recently as 1964, when the Welsh Office was created with a Minister in the British Cabinet.

The history of Scotland is very different, for it was a kingdom in its own right long before the union with England. Scotland was to a large extent unified in the eleventh century, although intermittent fighting between clans continued for some time afterwards. A Scottish Parliament sat in Edinburgh, and the country developed a legal system and a church that were quite distinct from their English equivalents. The legal system was particularly distinctive, being based on the principles of Roman law rather than on those of English common law. Scotland also developed an educational system that was in some respects superior to that in England and by the end of the sixteenth century it had four universities compared with England's two.

There was considerable rivalry between the English and the Scots and occasional border skirmishes. In the 1540s Henry VIII sent an expedition northwards, but this was withdrawn after Scotland entered into a defensive alliance with France and came under French protection. However, in 1603 James VI of Scotland was enthroned as James I of England and the two countries were on the road to unity, although for another century they had independent Parliaments and governments. In the 1690s there was a good deal of tension between the two governments, for the Scots sent an expedition to colonise a Central American territory which was then claimed by Spain and the English, to preserve their relations with Spain, effectively sabotaged the expedition. The Scottish Parliament refused to commit itself to the Hanoverian succession and in 1704 it passed an Act providing that on the death of Queen Anne the Scots would choose their own sovereign, who would not be the English monarch, unless Scotland were given adequate protection against English control of Scottish commerce.

The English Parliament retaliated with an Act which declared that after Christmas Day 1705 all trade between the two countries would be suspended and all Scotsmen in England would be treated as aliens, unless the Scots would appoint commissioners to enter into negotiations for a legislative union between the two countries. This threat had the desired effect and commissioners from both Parliaments subsequently agreed on a treaty of union. This treaty was unpopular with some sections of Scottish opinion and it was opposed by many English Tories, who objected to English recognition of the Presbyterian Church of Scotland. However, the treaty was enacted by a large majority in the Scottish Parliament in January 1707 and by the English Parliament two months later.

In retrospect, it can be seen that some such union was almost inevitable. Once the Scots had severed connections with the Catholic Church and ended their alliance with France, they had no effective allies to protect them against English dominance. It might have been costly for the English to conquer Scotland by armed force, but they were certainly ready to use their power to stamp on any commercial or diplomatic activities by the

Scots which conflicted with English interests. On the simple principle 'if you can't beat them, join them', it made sense for the educated and commercial classes of Scotland, enterprising and ambitious as they were, to join in political union with their more powerful and more prosperous neighbour. The English would not accept any half-way house between full union and separation, and the latter held few attractions. As a Scottish historian has said, 'it became clear to most Scots how hard it would be to refuse the union which England was pressing upon them without bringing down on themselves another era of chaos in the shape of internal division, dynastic war and commercial blockade' (Smout, pp. 215–16).

The union between England and Scotland was therefore very different in its origins from that between England and Wales, and it was also different in its consequences. Whereas Wales was completely integrated into the English (now British) governmental system, Scotland retained an independent legal system and a system of local government which was in some respects different from that in England. It also retained its own banking system and the right (which it has never lost) to issue its own bank-notes. The Presbyterian Church became the Church of Scotland and it was never proposed that the Church of England should become the established church north of the border, as it was in Wales until 1920.

The story in Ireland is more complicated but perhaps more familiar, partly because of the sporadic explosions of violence in that unhappy country and partly because Ireland, unlike Wales or Scotland, has been a major issue in British politics during much of the past century. Although English settlers had occupied lands around Dublin from the twelfth century onwards, it was not until the seventeenth century that substantial migration from the mainland took place. Following a successful military campaign in the western counties of Ulster against Irish lords who sought Spanish help, and who fled to the Continent when they were defeated, it was decided to confiscate the lands of these lords (and their neighbours) and to establish there a plantation for British settlers. The migrants to this plantation were for the most part plebeian rather than aristocratic in birth, Scottish rather than English in nationality, and Presbyterian rather than Anglican in religion. They were quickly followed by another group of Scottish settlers who acquired land in the two easternmost counties of Ulster, Antrim and Down; and 'within a generation a great part of both counties had been transformed, in population and way of life, into a sort of extension of the

Scottish lowlands' (Beckett (*b*), p. 47).

These settlers displaced the native-born and Roman Catholic peasants of the area, who in 1641 rose against the newcomers in what has come to be known as the Ulster Rising. This was a bloody affair which involved a massacre of Protestant settlers and which doubly weakened the Catholic Charles I. In the first place, the rebellion increased anti-Catholic feelings in England. Secondly, the need to finance a military expedition to put down the rising forced Charles to convene Parliament, which set in train the events leading to the English Civil War and eventually cost him his head. It also subjected both England and Ireland to the rule of Oliver Cromwell, who wreaked a terrible revenge on the Irish Catholics, killing many of their priests and destroying their churches and monasteries. There are elements of paradox and tragedy in this story which seem to thread their way through the history of Ireland right to the present day.

The restoration of the monarchy ended the persecution of Catholics and when James II acceded to the throne in 1685 there was a partial reversal of fortunes. Protestant officials lost office, an Irish army was recruited which was largely Catholic in composition, and for a short period it seemed as if the position of the Catholic Irish might be greatly improved. These hopes did not last long, for in the bloodless revolution of 1688 James fled from England without putting up a fight against William of Orange, his invading army and his English supporters. However, in Ireland only the small Protestant minority accepted William and Mary as legitimate rulers. In March 1689 James landed in Ireland from France and took command of the Irish army, and what was in effect a war for the English throne was then fought out on Irish soil. An attack on Londonderry was frustrated by the courage of the Protestant minority in the city – an event which has been celebrated annually ever since – and in July 1690 James came face to face with William in the Battle of the Boyne. In this famous encounter James's Irish and French troops were defeated by a mixed force of Ulster Protestants, Scots, Englishmen, Dutchmen and Danes, and this victory assured the supremacy of the Protestant religion in Britain. It also effectively quelled the resistance of the Irish Catholic population for a century.

During this century Ireland was governed by the Parliament in Dublin, which was monopolised by Protestant landowners since Catholics were not permitted either to sit in Parliament or to vote. This Parliament was notable for the 'Penal Laws' with which it discriminated against Catholics. Under these laws,

Catholics were not allowed to bear arms, Catholic priests were forbidden to celebrate Mass, and Catholics were not permitted to send their children abroad to be educated (to stop them going to Continental seminaries). To help Protestant landowners to extend their estates, it was decreed that Catholics could not buy land except on a short lease (up to 31 years) and could not bequeath their land by will. When a Catholic landowner died his land was divided equally between all his sons, which in a country of large families ensured the fragmentation of Catholic estates. As a final twist of the knife, it was decreed that if the eldest son of a Catholic landowner joined the Protestant Church, he would immediately be given ownership of the whole estate, with his father remaining simply as tenant for life and his brothers disinherited. And Catholics were barred from the army, the legal profession, and any kind of government or municipal office.

These measures effectively destroyed the position of the Catholic upper classes. Whereas in 1640 Catholics owned about 60 per cent of the country's land, by the 1730s this proportion had fallen to something like 5 per cent. The peasantry were rendered leaderless, except in so far as their remaining priests could lead them. Edmund Burke said that this period degraded the character of the Irish Catholic peasant, and a historian has elaborated the same view:

> His religion made him an outlaw . . . and whatever was inflicted on him he must bear, for where could he look for redress? To his landlord? Almost invariably an alien conqueror. To the law? Not when every person connected with the law, from the jailer to the judge, was a Protestant. . . .
>
> In these conditions suspicion of the law, of the ministers of the law and of all established authority worked into the very nerves and blood of the Irish peasant, and since the law did not give him justice he set up his own law. The secret societies which have been the curse of Ireland became widespread . . . dissimulation became a moral necessity and evasion of the law the duty of every God-fearing Catholic. (Woodham-Smith, pp. 27*ff*.)

The half-century following the Battle of the Boyne was the nadir of Irish history in terms of political and religious discrimination. In the second half of the eighteenth century the Penal Laws were gradually relaxed, and in 1793 (following pressure from London) the Catholics were enfranchised. As so often happens, reform encouraged fresh demands. The last years of the century saw the development of radical groups who were influenced by the political ideas of Rousseau and Tom Paine, and 1791 saw the formation of the United Irish Society, which numbered both Protestants and Catholics among its members and stood for independence from Britain.

In 1798, with French encouragement and a certain amount of French aid, the Society sponsored a rebellion against British rule in Ireland. The revolt was quickly and easily crushed but it was a sharp reminder of the threat to British security that Irish disaffection could pose, as Britain was then without allies in her war with France and could not easily contemplate the possibility of French bases being established in Ireland. The British reaction to this revolt was natural and perhaps inevitable: they persuaded their friends in the Irish Parliament to agree to an Act of Union whereby that Parliament was abolished and Ireland became an integral part of the United Kingdom.

The processes by which England's political authority was extended to include her Celtic neighbours were therefore very different. The union with Wales was the incorporation of a neighbouring territory accomplished without much apparent opposition from the people of that territory. The union with Scotland was brought about by treaty between two hitherto independent nations, made possible by the fact that they had a common king. The union with Ireland was a political takeover following centuries of conflict, conquest and oppression. In view of this history it is not surprising that the nationalist movements of the twentieth century in these countries should be very different in character.

Political Institutions and Conventions
When a national state is created by the union of one dominant country with several smaller countries, there are three obvious questions to ask about the political institutions of that state. First, are the smaller countries given adequate representation in the central organs of government? Secondly, are there special institutional arrangements to protect the particular interests and cultures of the smaller countries? Thirdly, is there a tradition of compromise and accommodation designed to instil confidence in the system on the part of the citizens of the smaller countries?

In terms of parliamentary representation, the smaller countries have done rather well. Wales has been treated in exactly the same way as England, the only difference being that in recent years Wales has had a few more parliamentary seats than the size of its electorate entitles it to. In 1977 Wales has 36 MPs although it would only have 31 if the average number of electors per constituency were the same as in England.

When the 1707 Act of Union was passed Scotland was given 45 seats out of 568 in the British Parliament, a number that was less than half what it would have been if it had been based on population but more than three times as great as it would have been if it had been based on taxation. Scottish representation was increased in 1832, 1867 and 1885 to a total of 72 seats, which was marginally more than its population entitled it to have. Since then the relative populations of the two countries have changed without any appreciable change in Scotland's representation, which should be 57 in terms of the English electoral quota but actually stands at 71.

When Ireland was incorporated into the United Kingdom it was given 100 seats, which was appreciably fewer than it would have had if the number had been based on population. But the reduction in the Irish population during the nineteenth century was not accompanied by any reduction in representation at Westminster, so that by the latter decades of the century Ireland was over-represented. In 1918 Ireland had 105 seats although representation by population would have entitled it to only 63 seats. As the Irish MPs were a constant embarrassment at Westminster from the 1880s onwards, this over-representation was a curious feature of the British political system of that period, just as the continued ability of citizens of the Irish Republic to vote in British elections is a curious feature of the contemporary political system.

The party affiliations of politicians in the three countries have of course varied, with the Welsh and Scots joining the main British parties and most of the Irish acting independently. Within the British parties Welsh and Scots politicians have achieved considerable influence, and it is to be noted that five of the seventeen Prime Ministers of the twentieth century have been Scots, while one has been Welsh. This is not an adequate guide to the influence of Welsh and Scottish MPs on government policy, but it shows that English politicians have not used their large majority to exclude the Welsh or the Scots from positions of power.

The achievements of the Irish Party at Westminster are of course a matter for debate. They repeatedly brought Irish problems to the attention of Parliament in the nineteenth century and they may be given part of the credit for some of the reforming legislation that was passed. It is also the case that the dependence of the Liberal Government on Irish support after the 1910 elections was one of the reasons for the introduction of the Home Rule Bill of 1912. But in the end the Irish reformers were frustrated by the Ulster Protestants and elbowed aside by nationalists of more militant disposition, who demanded independence rather than home rule and achieved their aim by violence rather than by parliamentary means.

The special institutional arrangements to safeguard the interests of the smaller countries have been minimal in the case of Wales, considerable in the case of Scotland, and larger still in the case of Ireland. Wales has been governed by all the laws that apply to England apart from a handful of special provisions, such as the Acts providing for local option in regard to Sunday opening of bars and cinemas in Wales. It was also administered in exactly the same way as England until 1964, when pressure from Welsh nationalists persuaded the Labour Government to introduce a form of administrative devolution for some public services.

The Scottish situation is more complicated. Most English legislation applies north of the Border, but there are a number of important matters on which separate legislation is required, including marriage and divorce, legal procedures, education and local government. There are also certain legislative reforms, such as the legalisation of homosexual relations between consenting adults, from which Scotland has been excluded in deference to the wishes of Scottish MPs.

In the administration of government services, special arrangements have been made for Scotland since the later years of the nineteenth century. Administrative control of prisons, the police, education, housing, public health and agriculture is now devolved to a group of government departments which are housed in Edinburgh. They all come under the political control of the Secretary of State for Scotland, a member of the British Cabinet who is responsible to Parliament for the devolved services. How far these special arrangements have safeguarded the particular interests of Scotland is of course the subject of lively debate.

In most important respects Ireland was treated as a separate entity during the period of formal integration, i.e. 1801–1921, with specific laws applicable only to Ireland being passed by the UK Parliament. The executive branch of government was headed by two British ministers known respectively as the Lord Lieutenant and First Secretary, but the executive departments for internal affairs were housed in Dublin rather than in London. It seems fair to say that the day-to-day government of Ireland was

conducted on a quasi-colonial basis in spite of its legal integration into the United Kingdom, the position being in some ways
analogous to the government of Algeria when it was part of
metropolitan France.

Because of this, and because Irish MPs were not included in
British parties or cabinets, Irish questions were always seen as
separate from British questions. Whereas Scotland and Wales
had influence in British government decision-making, Ireland
was a subject of British government decisions. And, although
in the latter part of the nineteenth century Westminster passed
many laws that benefited Ireland, the Irish always felt that they
were controlled by alien legislators who had little knowledge of
their country and little interest in it. In this the Irish were very
largely correct.

The third question posed at the beginning of this section is
whether the United Kingdom has a political tradition of compromise and accommodation designed for the benefit of the
smaller countries. The general answer to this must be in the
negative. Ireland has always been a special case, but Britain has
a very strong tradition of majoritarian government. Just as –
unlike most democracies – it has a 'first-past-the-post' system of
elections, so it has a firm convention that a government backed
by a parliamentary majority is entitled to do whatever it thinks
is in the national interest. There is no clear convention that on
some subjects special attention must be paid to Scottish or Welsh
opinion, such as exists in countries like Canada or Switzerland in
respect of their various regions.

Nor is there any convention that the composition of the
government should reflect the populations of the four countries
that constitute the kingdom. At the time of writing, the Cabinet
contains sixteen English ministers, four Welshmen and one
Scot, but the proportions vary from one Cabinet to another and
are not a subject of public comment. There is no expectation
that top civil service jobs should be shared around, and if there
are conventions about the distribution of patronage they are not
publicly known.

Of course, the Scots and the Welsh have some fairly effective
pressure groups and in some areas of policy they have done
better than English regions with similar problems. But this is
open to dispute and the point is that they compete with the
various English regions, not with England as a whole, and do so
within a system of conventions which are based on the assumption of complete political integration within Britain.

3
Nationalism and Political Integration

Nationalism

Like most terms ending in 'ism', the word 'nationalism' denotes a particular set of social and political beliefs. Although millions of words have been devoted to the history and character of these beliefs, their essence is not in serious dispute and can be captured most easily by defining the distinguishing qualities of a nationalist. In my view, a nationalist is best defined as a person who believes that the nation to which he belongs ought to govern itself (or to continue doing so); and that a debate about whether it would do so (or does so) efficiently is unnecessary because self-government is more important than efficient government. He may harbour other beliefs, ranging from the importance of sporting victories over other nations to the desirability of territorial expansion, but these are extensions of the doctrine rather than an essential part of it.

At face value this definition appears to be quite simple, but its clarity depends on the clarity of the key concept of 'nation'. Unfortunately this concept is far from clear, involving as it does a combination of political and social concepts. On the one hand, there is a set of terms like 'state', 'empire' and 'municipality' which refer to political institutions that can be identified by reference to legal documents. On the other hand, there is a set of terms like 'community', 'clan', 'tribe' and 'society' which refer to social groupings that have to be identified in terms of the attitudes, habits and relationships of their members. Although the term 'nation' is often used as if it belonged exclusively to either the former or the latter set, such usages disguise an essential feature of the concept of 'nation', which is that it straddles the gap between these two families of concepts. The most realistic short definition of a nation is that it is a society which either enjoys statehood or formerly enjoyed statehood or aspires to statehood. It follows that the identification of a nation involves both a discussion of social relationships and a discussion of political beliefs and institutions.

This inevitably leaves room for ambiguity and argument. In England, for example, almost everyone recognises that Scotland can properly be described as a nation, because although there is no Scottish state now there used to be one before 1707 and some national institutions have remained intact. Fewer Englishmen would concede that Wales should be so described, for although it has acquired one or two of the normal symbols of nationhood (such as football teams which play in international competitions) it has never enjoyed statehood and only a minority of Welshmen aspire to statehood. And no Englishman who is not Cornish would agree that Cornwall could reasonably be described as a nation, though Cornish nationalists make similar claims to Welsh nationalists and the latter accept the Cornish claim to nationhood. Similar ambiguities can be discerned in other countries which are composed of one dominant group and several minorities. Examples include Spanish attitudes to the Basques and Catalonians, French attitudes to Bretons and Corsicans, Turkish attitudes to the Kurds and English-Canadian attitudes to the Quebecois.

To analyse the ambiguous concepts of nation and nationalism, it is essential to specify the various ways in which they can be identified and examined. I believe that a useful first step is to distinguish three separate factors which are involved in any national or nationalist movement, as follows:

(1) the social bases of nationalism;
(2) the political conditions for the growth of nationalism;
(3) the time-reference of nationalism.

(1) By 'the social bases of nationalism' I mean the forces that bind the members of the national society together and give them a sense of group identity and group loyalty. In Pakistan and Israel religion is the social basis of nationalism. In other countries race or ethnicity fill this role. In Quebec language and culture are the bases of the nationalist movement. In many countries, including England and France, nationalism is based on a feeling of social unity that has developed over many centuries, although the English and French peoples are of varied ethnic origin and follow more than one religion.

(2) The existence of positive feelings of national identity, whatever their social basis, is one of the necessary conditions for the emergence of nationalism. Other things being equal, a positive correlation may be expected between the strength of the feelings of national identity and the strength of nationalist beliefs and loyalties. However, this is only half the story. The other neces-

sary condition is the recognition of rivals or enemies whose activities threaten the welfare of the national community or society. The emergence of Italian nationalism in the nineteenth century depended not only on the development of a sense of national identity – a belief that 'we are all Italians and should therefore be united' – but also on the recognition of common enemies, namely the French and the Austrians. And there also tends to be a positive correlation between the extent to which the national society feels itself threatened and the intensity of nationalist feelings. Countries at war invariably experience a surge of nationalism, and Israel is an outstanding example of a society in which the strength of nationalist feelings owes more to the constant threat posed by its neighbours than to the social and cultural unity of its people.

(3) By 'the time-reference of nationalism' I do not mean the number of years or the exact historical period in which nationalist feelings developed but the question of whether national state-hood – the focus of these feelings – is located in the past, the present or the future. Most nationalist movements and parties are future-oriented and this kind of movement can best be called 'aspiring nationalism'. Nationalist feelings on the part of citizens of a national state can appropriately be called 'possessive nationalism'. Nationalist movements by groups who have lost their state or have been driven from their territory are examples of 'dispossessed nationalism'.

Now, it is a matter of common experience that people feel more strongly when something they value is taken from them or threatened than they do about things they desire but have never yet enjoyed. For this reason, dispossessed nationalism tends to burn with the fiercest flame of these three categories, the obvious contemporary example being the nationalism of the Palestine Liberation Organisation and the feelings of the neighbouring Arab states who believe that Israel occupies Arab lands. Posses-sive nationalism is rarely as fierce as this, except when seriously threatened (as in the case of Israel), but it has the strength and inertia of established institutions and traditions to support it. Aspiring nationalism is usually the weakest of the three, and is unlikely to acquire a mass following unless the dedication of its leaders (usually educated and visionary men) is supplemented by some dramatic turn of events which captures the imagination of ordinary people who are not normally inclined to support vision-ary political movements. This turn of events may be called 'the eruptive factor', its distinguishing feature being not its inherent character (for this may vary widely) but its consequences for the nationalist movement. Thus, the eruptive factor which generated widespread international support for the Zionist Movement was Hitler's extermination of millions of Jews; the eruptive factor for Irish nationalism was the execution of the leaders of the Easter Rising; and the Scottish equivalent was the discovery of North Sea oil.

Armed with these simple analytical tools, it is fairly easy to identify some of the strengths and weaknesses of the various forms of nationalism within the British Isles. Thus, the weaknesses of Irish nationalism in the nineteenth century were, first, that it was an aspiring nationalism facing the possessive nationalism of the British and, secondly, that although it had a conspicuous enemy it lacked an adequate sense of unity, pride and achievement to serve as a positive focus of loyalty. The main strength of Ulster nationalism, in contrast, has been its possessive nature, clearly reflected in slogans like 'no surrender' and 'what we have we hold'. Ulster nationalism did not need an 'eruptive factor' to generate mass support, though it was not until the vital interests of the Ulster Protestants were threatened that their solidarity and determination became apparent to the outside world. One of the strengths of Scottish nationalism, as compared with Welsh, is the history of Scottish statehood and the pride the Scots take in their distinctive institutions. On the other hand, Welsh nationalism derives some of its passion from a feeling of dispossession – not, indeed, of political institutions but of the Welsh language and culture, long in decline and recently threatened with virtual extinction. All these and many related matters will be explored in subsequent chapters, together with the slightly mysterious phenomenon of English nationalism.

There is, however, another and wider form of identity and loyalty within the British Isles, which is attached to the United Kingdom as a long-established state. The analysis of this is beset with semantic and other difficulties. If it were simply loyalty to the Crown and the institutions of this state, it would be correctly described as 'patriotism', so that one could distinguish English nationalism from British or UK patriotism. But it is not so simple as that. Because the process of social and political integration has been fairly successful, these two types of loyalty are indistinguishable in most citizens' minds. There is clearly a sense of British nationhood and British nationalism which is shared by all the English and most of the Scots and Welsh, though it does not include the Unionists of Northern Ireland. Their loyalty is to the Crown and state rather than to Britain as a social entity and their attitudes will be examined in Chapter 4.

Leaving Northern Ireland on one side, there are some awkward semantic difficulties about the term 'British'. This is the adjectival form of two distinct nouns, namely 'Britain' the place and 'Britons' the people. Unfortunately the latter term is pedantic and very rarely used. Americans have filled the ensuing void by coining the word 'Britisher', but although this is logical the word is extremely ugly to British ears and is never used outside America.

A further complication is that the term 'British' is also used as a form of shorthand to describe a legal category, namely 'British subject', which category includes (or has until very recently included) several hundred million people in various parts of the Commonwealth. When I visited Nigeria in its colonial days, before there was any real sense of Nigerian nationhood, I was intrigued to discover that people there characteristically identified themselves as Ibos, Yorubas, etc., or British, and referred to white people from Britain living in Nigeria as 'expatriates'. (Because of these linguistic ambiguities it was also common to describe Britain as UK and British-educated Africans as people who had been to UK – in shorthand, 'been-tos'. As a locally educated Yoruba told me: 'All the best jobs go to expatriates and been-tos.')

The English themselves get over these difficulties by a method which the Scots and the Welsh regard as characteristically arrogant. This method is to treat the words 'English' and 'British' as interchangeable and to use the former more frequently, so that in common parlance the word 'English' is generally meant to include the Scots and the Welsh. This usage is a minor source of irritation to the latter, particularly since it has been adopted in many European countries so that Scottish or Welsh tourists in Italy or Spain find themselves described as 'Inglese' or 'Inglés'. This brief excursion into semantics illustrates some of the problems of political integration in a multinational state.

Political Integration

Political integration may be loosely defined as the process by which local communities are not only brought within the control of a larger state but also submerge their local loyalties into feelings of loyalty and support for the larger unit. This process has also been described as national integration or nation-building, and objections can be made to each of the three terms. The problem about 'nation-building' is that it seems to exclude the possibility of a stable multinational state. The difficulty about 'national integration' is that, as Claude Ake has said, it seems to be tautological (Ake, p. 14). The difficulty about 'political integration' is that, if narrowly defined, it would exclude the cultural, social and economic factors which are involved in the process. I propose to get around these difficulties by using the last term in a broad way so as to include the social and other factors which contribute to (or hinder) the development of integration.

Social scientists concerned with the problems of political integration have produced two contrasting models of development, for each of which predictive value has been claimed. One of these models has been popular throughout the present century and supported, with varying emphasis, by such scholars as Max Weber, Ferdinand Tonnies, Talcott Parsons, S. M. Lipset, Stein Rokkan and Karl Deutsch. According to this model, the cultural differences between the core and the peripheral regions of a nation-state will be gradually broken down by the consequences of industrialisation, personal mobility, mass communications and the increasing activities of the national government. As the whole country becomes 'modernised', local loyalties and cultures will lose their significance and political conflict will come to be based simply on national economic rivalries between classes and interest groups.

This model is supported by a great deal of evidence and the only trouble with it is that its predictions have not always come true. As noted above, the United Kingdom is by no means the only industrialised state in which local loyalties and cultures have survived and are now threatening the stability of the regime. Largely because of this, a new model has recently been devised, known as 'internal colonialism'. According to this model, the relations between the core and peripheral regions of a state are essentially exploitative (see Gonzales-Casanova; Stavenhagen; and Hechter). The core region dominates the peripheral regions, which is resented by the latter, and sooner or later separatist movements develop as a reaction to this domination. Of the exponents of this model, only Michael Hechter has yet published a substantial book on the subject. According to him, the two central features of the system of exploitation are as follows: (1) the dominant group defines and regulates recruitment to positions of high prestige in the state so as to exclude individuals from the peripheral areas; (2) peripheral industrialisation is controlled by the dominant group so as to ensure that it is highly specialised and dependent on export markets (see Hechter, pp. 9 and 10).

Unfortunately for this model, there is no evidence that either of these features can be found in the United Kingdom. Positions of high prestige and influence are commonly filled by Scotsmen, Welshmen and Irishmen: in government and the civil service by members of all three nations; in industry, banking and the medical profession by Scotsmen; in the learned professions by Welshmen; and in the armed forces by Irishmen. The degree of industrial specialisation varies from one region to another, and A. J. Brown has worked out 'co-efficients of specialisation' based on the distribution of employment in 1966. These show that Northern Ireland and the West Midlands were the most highly specialised of the eleven standard regions (with co-efficients of 20·4 in each case); that Wales was slightly more specialised than the average region (14·7 compared with the mean co-efficient of 13·9); but that Scotland (co-efficient 8·9) was less specialised than any other region (Brown, p. 40). These figures do not support the model of internal colonialism, which is more seriously misleading than the 'functionalist' or 'diffusionist' model which it seeks to replace.

Since the study of politics can never be an exact science, it is best to abandon the search for a predictive model and to content ourselves with a list of factors which either contribute to the process of political integration or hinder it. The main factors which contribute to the development of political integration may be summarised as follows:

(1) the development of a common language, national educational system and national mass media;
(2) the growth of personal interaction and mobility between different regions;
(3) the development of national political parties with centralised forms of organisation;
(4) the growth of an integrated economic system with features (natural or artificial) which ensure that all regions share to some extent in the benefits of economic growth.

The main factors which hinder political integration are:

(1) the persistence of ethnic, religious or linguistic divisions between regions;
(2) economic imbalance between the regions, of a type which may lead residents of the poorer areas to feel that they are being unfairly treated.

Before discussing these factors, it will be convenient to set out a few basic statistics about the constituent territories of the

British Isles (excluding the Channel Islands and the Isle of Man), and this is done in Table 3.1.

Table 3.1 *The Constituent Territories in 1971*

Territory	Popula-tion millions	Persons per sq. mile	Relative GDP per head* (UK= 100)	Workers in agricul-ture %	Roman Catholics %	Speak-ing a Gaelic lan-guage %
England	45·9	915	103	3	10	—
Scotland	5·2	175	89	5	16	1·5
Wales	2·7	341	86	5	7	21
Northern Ireland ..	1·5	292	72	10	35	—
Republic of Ireland	3·0	108	62	31	95	27

*GDP=Gross Domestic Product

Language, Education and the Mass Media

It is not generally realised that in the first decade of the nineteenth century about a fifth of the people of the United Kingdom spoke one or other of the three Gaelic languages as their first or only language. This linguistic minority included about nine-tenths of Welsh people, half of the Irish and just under a quarter of the Scots. These languages were derived from the two main versions of Gaelic, known to modern linguists as q-Gaelic and p-Gaelic. The former was spoken by the Catholic population of Ireland and (with slight variations) by the people of the Scottish Highlands and the Western Isles. The Highlanders and Islanders were mainly descended from the Scots, an Irish tribe who had crossed the water and settled in those areas during the Dark Ages. P-Gaelic was spoken by the Welsh and (with some variations) by many of the people living in Cornwall.

In all areas government was in the hands of English-speaking peoples, who have attempted to eliminate the speaking of Gaelic with varying degrees of determination and success. In the small county of Cornwall the English completely extinguished Gaelic during the nineteenth century, so that recent attempts by Cornish separatists to re-create the language have been artificial as well as unsuccessful. In Scotland the English-speaking Lowlanders have been politically dominant since early modern times, and 'it was Lowland policy . . . to destroy the Gaelic language in the interest of national unity' (Kermack, pp. 152–3). During the early part of the eighteenth century the Scottish authorities forbade the teaching of Gaelic in their schools, and this policy was pursued with sufficient determination to result in the virtual disappearance of the language on the Scottish mainland, though it still survives in the Western Isles.

In Wales the 1536 Act made English the language of government, and as it also became the main language of commerce and industry the townsfolk of Wales became English-speakers. In 1846 a British government report on education contained some highly derogatory passages about the uselessness of the Welsh language and the desirability of its disappearance, and for some years after 1870 children were liable to be punished if they were heard speaking Welsh while in school. Nevertheless, in the rural areas the chapels and chapel schools resisted this policy and succeeded in keeping the language alive, so that in 1901 15 per cent of the population spoke only Welsh and 35 per cent claimed to speak both Welsh and English. During the present century, although educational attitudes have become much more liberal, the use of the language has gradually declined. The 1931 census showed that 96 per cent of the population could speak English and this had risen to 99 per cent by 1961. The proportion claiming to speak Welsh fell from 37 per cent in 1931 to 21 per cent in 1971. In the two most industrialised counties, containing 63 per cent of the population, only 9 per cent could speak Welsh in 1971. There are no daily newspapers published in Welsh, and television programmes are almost entirely in English.

The six counties of Northern Ireland have become entirely English-speaking, and in the twenty-six counties which now form the Republic English has been the dominant language since the eighteenth century. The 1911 census showed that only 18 per cent of the population of the twenty-six counties claimed to speak Gaelic and although the Republic has made determined efforts to revive the language its success has been very limited.

The almost universal use of the English language has been an integrative factor not only because it facilitates personal communication and commerce but also because it gives everyone access to the same literature and the same textbooks. And the economics of the publishing industry have ensured that the overwhelming majority of textbooks are English not only in language but in outlook. However, the educational systems themselves have not been completely integrated. The Scottish educational system has always been unique, and it is quite exceptional for children from Scottish schools to go to universities outside Scotland. The Irish educational systems are also different and have been sharply divided on religious lines, nearly all schools having affiliations with either the Protestant or Catholic Churches. As in Scotland, virtually all Irish students stay in their own country for their university education. Welsh state schools (as distinct from chapel schools) have been fully integrated into the English educational system, just as Welsh local government has. Since church and chapel schools in Wales and England were taken over by the state under the 1944 Education Act, all Welsh schools (apart from a handful of private ones) are now run on the same lines as English schools. Their pupils take the same examinations and a majority of the Welsh school-leavers who go on to university now do so in England. In return, a fair number of English school-leavers attend the University of Wales and comprise a majority of the students of that University. The figures are given in Table 3.2. However, in recent years an increasing number of Welsh secondary schools have included the teaching of Welsh in their syllabus and have even made it a compulsory subject. This is a divisive development which will be discussed in Chapter 7.

Table 3.2 *Country of Domicile and Location of University Education in December 1974*

Country of Domicile	Location of University Education			
	England '000	Wales '000	Scotland '000	N. Ireland '000
England	134·3	7·8	4·6	0·3
Wales	4·9	4·5	0·1	—
Scotland	1·5	—	28·0	—
Northern Ireland ...	1·6	0·1	0·5	5·8

Source: Universities Statistical Record

Turning to the mass media, we find a pattern rather similar to the educational one. The Irish Republic has its own press, and in Northern Ireland the number of people who read British newspapers is much smaller than the number who subscribe to Belfast papers. In England and Wales the press is highly centralised, as virtually everyone reads one or other of the eight national newspapers that are produced in London. Local and regional papers are read in addition to national papers rather than as alternatives to them, and people generally look to the London papers for political news and to their local papers for local gossip and cinema programmes. The Cardiff-based *Western Mail* is the only Welsh daily paper which attempts to be an alternative to the national press, but its circulation of 95,000 hardly rivals a circulation in Wales of the London daily papers of over 600,000. The position in Scotland is appreciably different in that the total circulation of the Scottish-based daily papers is about the same as that of the London-based papers, and the Scottish editions of the latter contain a high proportion of Scottish news.

Radio and television are also highly centralised in the United Kingdom. The BBC has four radio programmes, all produced in London and divided on cultural rather than regional lines. They can be characterised as highbrow, middlebrow, lowbrow and pop, and they all carry the same national news bulletins with the addition of short regional news items on one (but only one) of the channels. The two BBC television channels also cover the whole country with only minor variations. The main news programmes are nationwide, and it is only in the early evening from Monday to Friday that the national news is supplemented by a short programme of regional news. This, however, causes controversy in Wales as this regional bulletin is now given in Welsh and is therefore incomprehensible to 80 per cent of viewers. The fifteen independent television companies vary somewhat in their programmes, but if one ignores the random differences between their choices of old movies it is clear that over four-fifths of their viewing time is given over to the same material. They all show three news programmes each day produced in London by Independent Television News and supplement this with two short programmes of regional news. The Welsh independent channel broadcasts in Welsh for an average period of just under an hour a day, avoiding peak viewing hours.

The data given in this section reinforce one another. The mass media in Britain, particularly the press, are far more centralised than they are in most countries of comparable population. In most respects the Welsh media and educational system are indistinguishable from the English. In Scotland and Northern Ireland both the educational systems and the press are different, but television and radio are much the same as they are in England. In all areas and all media the news items place a very considerable emphasis on the activities of the government in London.

Personal Interaction and Mobility
As most people travelling any appreciable distance in Britain go by train, the best guide to personal movements is the railway timetable. This confirms the dominance of London as the political, commercial and industrial capital of Britain. Even though it is in the extreme south-east of the country, the number of inter-city trains going to and from London greatly exceeds the number

plying between other cities. In Scotland there is a shuttle service between Glasgow and Edinburgh (only 45 miles apart) but London is otherwise the main destination. In Wales the great majority of long-distance trains from Cardiff go to London, and while there is also a good deal of short-distance traffic across the border in an east–west direction there is little traffic between south Wales and north Wales. It takes two hours to travel from Cardiff (the capital) to London but five hours to get from Cardiff to Aberystwyth, where the National Library of Wales is situated.

Table 3.3   *Number of Inter-city Express Trains Each Day (1975)*

Between London and:					
Edinburgh	24	Manchester	32	Liverpool	24
Glasgow	18	Sheffield	34	Birmingham	60
Newcastle	42*	Leeds	26	Cardiff	40
Bristol	46	Southampton	56	Exeter	28
Between other cities:					
Glasgow and Edinburgh		66	Liverpool and Leeds		18
Glasgow and Liverpool		4	Manchester and Bristol		4
Glasgow and Manchester		4	Manchester and Cardiff		6
Glasgow and Birmingham		4	Birmingham and Cardiff		10
			Belfast and Dublin		8

*This figure is inflated by the fact that most London–Edinburgh trains stop at Newcastle, but this is the only example of double counting in the table.

These figures illustrate not only the degree of centralisation within Britain but also the very large volume of passenger traffic between London and the other main cities of the country. It is reasonable to assume that the average train carries about 300 passengers, and on this assumption about 18,000 people must travel between Birmingham and London by rail each day, about 9,000 in each direction. Figures for the other cities are easy to calculate. A fairly high proportion of these passengers are business executives and public officials who go up to the capital on the morning trains to transact business in government departments or company head offices, returning to their homes in the evening. There is also a fair sprinkling of housewives bound for London shops, so that for some sections of the middle classes (but not for manual workers) much of England has some of the qualities of a London suburb. This degree of centralisation naturally strengthens the social and political integration of England, while it weakens regional loyalties.

Table 3.4 gives approximate figures for passenger movement by rail, sea and air across national borders within the British Isles.

Since it is impossible to secure even rough estimates of the volume of road traffic the figures are of limited importance, but two points nevertheless emerge quite clearly. The first is that there is much more personal movement between Wales and England than there is between Scotland and England – three times as much if allowance is made for the relative populations of Scotland and Wales. The second point is that, when allowance is made for their respective populations, travel between the Republic of Ireland and Britain is just as great as travel between Northern Ireland and Britain.

Table 3.4 *Estimated Passenger Movements by Rail, Sea and Air in 1975*

Between Scotland and England	*c.*	6 million
Between Wales and England	*c.*	9 million
Between Northern Ireland and Britain	*c.*	1·6 million
Between the Republic of Ireland and Britain	*c.*	3·3 million

Statistics for telephone calls and letter traffic show similar trends. In 1974–5 there were 25·5 million telephone calls from Wales to England but only 21·3 million telephone calls from Scotland to England, although Scotland has almost twice the population of Wales. In 1975 2·04 per cent of all inland letter traffic was from Wales to England whereas only 1·93 per cent was from Scotland to England. The figures regarding letter traffic provide another measure of the greater isolation of Scotland. In the seven English regions 51 per cent of letters were sent to addresses within the region; in Wales 54 per cent of the letters posted were sent to addresses within Wales; but in Scotland 72 per cent of letters were sent to Scottish addresses. The figures also illustrate the central position of London, for in Scotland, Wales and each of the six English provincial regions London was the most common destination of letters sent outside the region and the proportion of mail sent to London (26 per cent of all non-local mail) was much higher than the proportion of the British population living in London (13 per cent).

National Political Parties
The Conservative and Labour Parties treat Wales as if it were a region of England. The Labour Party treats Scotland in the same way, so that the Scottish Regional Council of the Labour

Party has no more powers than, say, the Regional Council for South–West England. The National Union of Conservative and Unionist Associations does not cover Scotland, so that the Scottish Association has its own independent existence and its own annual conference. The Liberal Party has separate organisations in both Scotland and Wales.

The parties in Northern Ireland have never been integrated with those on the mainland. For many years the Ulster Unionist Party had close associations with the Conservative Party but this era came to an end when the Conservative Government suspended the Stormont Parliament in 1972. The Labour Party used to have fraternal links with the Northern Ireland Labour Party, but this latter organisation was always very small. There are no clear links between the Labour Party and the Social Democratic and Labour Party (SDLP) that was established in Belfast in 1970, but some SDLP leaders enjoy friendly relations with some Labour MPs, both front-bench and back-bench.

Economic Integration

Given an industrial economy, the most conspicuous benefit of political unity is the rapid economic growth that is made possible by a large market and the concentration of different types of industry in the most suitable areas. The political unity of the British Isles facilitated the growth of industry and in the late eighteenth and the nineteenth centuries the rewards of economic growth were probably the most important of the factors aiding political and social integration.

The Industrial Revolution was accompanied by a large-scale movement of population from the countryside to the towns, but as the centres of industrial growth (clustered mainly near coalfields and the major ports) were scattered around Britain there was not a great deal of regional imbalance. In England all regions shared in the prosperity. In the Scottish Lowlands fortunes were made out of shipbuilding and engineering, and south Wales was transformed by the development of the mining, steel and tinplate industries. The middle classes were highly conscious of their good fortune and it became common to talk of 'Great Britain', with a certain emphasis on the first word. Among the Scottish bourgeoisie it became fashionable to refer to their country not as Scotland but as 'North Britain'. The financiers and engineers who built the first railway in Scotland called it the North British Railway, and to this day the massive North British Hotel stands in the centre of Edinburgh as a monument to that mode of thought. Ireland has no minerals, but the linen industry was developed in Belfast and the city later became a major shipbuilding centre, with materials imported from Britain.

The only areas left out of this process of industrialisation were the areas of cultural minorities – the Scottish Highlands, northern and western Wales, and Catholic Ireland. The consequence was large-scale emigration – from the Highlands to the Lowlands (and to England and overseas), from north and west Wales to south Wales and England, from Ireland to England, Scotland and North America. In Catholic Ireland it could be said that another consequence was grinding poverty, but this was caused by a number of factors apart from the lack of industry.

Since 1920 the impact of economic forces has been different. The decline of the textile industries, shipbuilding and mining has impoverished many of the older industrial areas, while the new industries (fuelled by oil and electricity) have developed mainly in the southern half of England. Ever since 1920, unemployment rates in Scotland, Wales, Northern Ireland and parts of northern England have been appreciably higher than the rates in southern England. This geographical imbalance has led to regional grievances which have been articulated by local trade unionists and politicians. However, these grievances have been aggregated by the Labour Party, which has always favoured a policy of political and administrative centralisation. From the early twenties onwards, the Labour Party (supported by the Trades Union Congress) discouraged direct action, local initiatives, workers' control and all similar policies in favour of national (meaning United Kingdom) economic planning, the reduction of inequality by the use of national taxes, and the development of social services under central control.

This attitude by the Labour Party and the unions clearly helped to maintain political stability and integration. It also brought political success to the party, which gained both an image of respectability and the normal support of the majority of Scottish, Welsh and northern English electors. Finally, it is clear that the centralised character of British government, which Labour has encouraged, has brought economic benefits to the poorer regions.

The basic principles involved are simple. In a common market, with free movement of labour and capital, there are always differential rates of economic growth. If there is no central administration to compensate the slow-growing areas they may be worse off than they would have been if they had remained outside the market. Thus, it has been shown that the East African Common Market brought large benefits to Kenya, marginal benefits to

Uganda, and a substantial loss to Tanganyika (see Ghai). In a federal system the poorer states benefit to some extent from fiscal equalisation but the standard of public services is apt to vary from state to state (see Birch; May). But in a centralised system of government social services of a uniform standard are normally provided over the whole country, which means that the wealthier regions automatically subsidise the others through the fiscal system.

This is certainly the case in the United Kingdom, where residents of poorer countries and regions contribute less than average to government revenues but enjoy public services that are more expensive than average. Some relevant figures are given in Tables 3.5 and 3.6 – for particular years only because official statistics are not normally broken down on a geographical basis.

Table 3.5   *The Difference between Tax Receipts and Beneficial Government Expenditures by Region in 1964*

Region	Relative GDP per head	Beneficial Government Expenditures minus Tax Receipts
	% of UK figure	£ per head
South East	113	− 39
West Midlands	109	− 22
Yorkshire and Humberside ...	99	+ 13
North West	98	+ 5
East Midlands	98	+ 14
South West	88	+ 25
Wales	88	+ 45
East Anglia	87	+ 37
Scotland	86	+ 32
North	85	+ 31
Northern Ireland	66	+ 82

Source: Commission on the Constitution, Research Paper 10, p. 72.

Since the Second World War the peripheral regions have also benefited from government policies designed to diversify their industrial structure. This represents a change of policy, as between the wars grants were given towards industrial retraining and the cost of moving so as to facilitate the movement of workers from the areas of high unemployment in the north and west of Great Britain into the areas of industrial growth in the midlands and south-east. The grants were not really adequate but they did contribute towards mobility and towards the rapid growth of new industrial towns, such as Slough, Luton and

Table 3.6 *Central Government Expenditures on Local Services by Region in 1968–9*

Region	Expenditure per head as % of English total
South East	96
West Midlands	93
Yorkshire and Humberside ...	100
North West	107
East Midlands	92
South West	95
Wales	130
East Anglia	96
Scotland	142
North	133

Source: Commission on the Constitution, Research Paper 10, p. 9.

Dagenham (all within 30 miles of London). Between 1928 and 1938, about 280,000 people of working age were assisted to move by the Industrial Transference Board (Brown, p. 281). However, the Barlow Report of 1942 recommended that a policy of moving jobs to the people would be socially and economically more desirable than the policy of moving people to jobs, and both the main political parties have accepted this view.

The instruments of this 'regional policy' have included differential investment grants, differential investment allowances, differential taxes on employers, the construction of factory buildings by the government in areas of high unemployment to be let at low rentals, and the use of government controls over industrial and office building to prevent the expansion of industrial activities in the more prosperous areas of the country. Thus, the Ford Motor Company was refused permission to extend its integrated plant at Dagenham and was forced to accommodate its expansion in a new plant in the Liverpool area, even though this meant that components had to be transported over 200 miles. Equally, Chrysler (formerly Rootes) was not allowed to extend its plant in Coventry and had to expand by building a new factory near Glasgow, about 300 miles away.

These policies were pursued vigorously by the Labour Government of 1945–51, less vigorously by the Conservative Governments of the following decade, and with renewed vigour since 1962. To some extent the policies have achieved their aims. They have helped to prevent the decay of certain older industrial areas and they have reduced the scale of the movement of population towards the midlands and the south-east. However, they have had only a small impact on the differences in the level of unemployment, as is indicated by Table 3.7.

Table 3.7   *Regional Unemployment Levels (Annual Averages)*

Region	1965 %	1969 %	1972 %	1974 %
Northern England	2·5	4·8	6·3	4·7
Yorkshire and Humberside	1·1	2·6	4·2	2·8
East Midlands	0·9	1·9	3·1	2·2
East Anglia	1·3	1·9	2·9	2·0
South East	0·8	1·5	2·1	1·6
South West	1·5	2·7	3·5	2·7
West Midlands	0·7	1·8	3·6	*
North West	1·6	2·4	4·8	3·5
Wales	2·5	4·0	5·2	3·8
Scotland	2·9	3·7	6·4	4·1
Northern Ireland	6·0	7·1	8·2	6·0
United Kingdom	1·5	2·5	3·8	2·7

*This figure is not available because of industrial action at the Employment Service Agency.
Source: Annual Abstract of Statistics, 1975

Moreover, the costs of this kind of regional policy have been extremely high. The use of government controls and public money to induce employers to site their factories in areas which they would not choose on economic grounds is bound to reduce the overall rate of economic growth. The cost to the midlands has been particularly high. For instance, it is reported that the division of Chrysler's plants between Coventry and Scotland has added appreciably to the cost of each vehicle produced, which must have contributed to the collapse of the company in the mid-seventies. In the booming fifties it may perhaps have been plausible to suggest that the prosperous midlands could afford to subsidise Scotland and the northern counties of England, but it is hardly plausible now that three of the biggest concerns in the midlands (Rolls Royce, British Leyland and Chrysler) have collapsed and are only kept going by subsidies from the taxpayer. The once-extensive motor-cycle industry of the midlands has also collapsed and the profitable sections of the aircraft manufacturing industry are outweighed by the massive public subsidies for the production of Concorde, which can never be a success in economic terms.

The ultimate logic of these postwar regional policies is that the taxpayers and business concerns of London and the Home Counties should subsidise the rest of the United Kingdom. But instead of planning for an orderly expansion of London (as French governments have planned for the expansion of Paris), town planning controls and other government measures have been used with the deliberate object of producing a contraction. The consequences include a serious housing shortage, a labour shortage in organisations like London Transport, and an astronomical rise in the cost of commuting. Over the past twenty years some aspects of the quality of life in the London area have clearly deteriorated, while in Paris they have conspicuously improved.

This in itself is unlikely to worry people outside London, but they should be concerned about the economic consequences of a decline in the size of the country's most prosperous city. London is not only the leading centre of finance, banking and insurance, which earn large amounts of foreign exchange, but is also an industrial city. It is the largest centre of electronic and electrical engineering in the country and is also a major centre for the production of motor-vehicle parts, clothing, films and records, and a wide variety of specialised goods. As a result of official policies its population declined from 8 million to 7 million between 1946 and 1976 and will be down to 6 million by 1990 unless policies are changed. This makes Britain the only industrial country in the world which is deliberately reducing the size of what could be its leading centre of economic growth. Carried to this extreme, British regional policies are slowly but surely throttling the geese that lay the golden eggs. Ironically, the policies have not even produced the political gratitude that was expected, as the voters of Scotland (which has benefited more than any other region) are now deserting the two main parties to support the Scottish National Party.

Another aspect of economic integration that deserves brief mention is the extent to which the industrial activities of the various regions are interdependent. As over 80 per cent of freight traffic in Britain goes by road, the statistics for road freight transport offer the best simple guide to this matter. The last official survey was made in 1967–8, showing the region of origin and the destination of freight. This survey indicated that Wales is so closely integrated with England that, in economic terms, it can reasonably be regarded as a part of it. In the nine regions of England, inter-regional freight traffic, expressed as a proportion of intra-regional traffic, varied from 32 per cent in the North to 59 per cent in the West Midlands, the average for all the regions being approximately 40 per cent. The equivalent proportion for Wales was exactly 40 per cent (Road Transport Survey). In Scotland the equivalent proportion was only 14 per cent.

If railway freight is added, it appears that the total freight traffic between England and Wales in the early seventies was approximately 46,000,000 tons a year, while freight traffic between England and Scotland was only about 24,000,000 tons a year. These figures reinforce the figures given earlier about personal mobility between the three countries. Freight traffic by sea between Britain and the Irish Republic amounted to about 10,000,000 tons in 1971 and that between Britain and Northern Ireland amounted to about 7,000,000 tons. Traffic across the land border in Ireland amounted to 1,200,000 tons (see Freight Transport Statistics). These figures also reinforce the statistics given earlier about personal movement: it seems clear that the independent political status of the Republic has had relatively little effect on the extent of trade and personal mobility between Ireland and Britain.

Limitations to Political Integration
Foreign scholars have sometimes asked why English politicians have been so much less successful in developing political integration between their country and Ireland than between England, Wales and Scotland. The data presented in this chapter go a long way towards answering this question even without an examination of the vagaries of Anglo-Irish political relationships. The educational system and mass media of Ireland have always been different from those of England; the Irish Sea has reduced the level of personal interaction; Irish political parties have always been independent; and, apart from a fairly small area around Belfast, Ireland has not shared in the prosperity that followed the rapid growth of British industry in the nineteenth century. The whole of Ireland has been and is a rather backward appendage to Britain, and although there are good reasons for the continued constitutional links between Northern Ireland and Great Britain the social and economic bases for full integration between the countries just do not exist.

In the case of Wales all the social and economic factors that help to develop integration have been present, apart from the survival of the Welsh language in some areas of the country. This is an important reservation and it is also important that Welsh people have feelings of Welsh identity, combined perhaps with certain cultural characteristics, that mark them off from their English neighbours. These factors will be explored in

Chapter 7. But it remains true that, by all objective indicators, Wales is highly integrated with England.

Scotland's position lies somewhere between that of Ireland and that of Wales. Scotland's economic system is more self-contained than that of Wales; its educational and legal systems are uniquely Scottish; its mass media differ significantly from those of England; and the level of personal interaction between Scotland and England is lower than that between Wales and England. For over two centuries the Scottish people have been content to accept political direction from the UK Parliament and government, so that the degree of political integration between Scotland and England has been fairly high in spite of these differences. However, the recent growth of a party dedicated to Scottish independence, and all the possibilities of disintegration that this produces, will be examined in later chapters.

But since we already have one practical example of political disintegration within the British Isles it is clearly appropriate to see what lessons can be learnt from this before we examine the aspiring nationalist movements of Scotland and Wales. For this reason the next two chapters will be devoted to Ireland.

4

Ireland: Nationalism and Its Consequences

There are one or two general observations to be made about nationalism in Ireland before the development and ideas of its nationalist movements are considered in detail. Since the country was governed in a colonial fashion from the twelfth century onwards, and had never existed as an independent state, an Irish nationalist movement had to be aspiring in character rather than possessive. Now, nationalist movements of an aspiring kind are invariably founded by educated middle-class groups, not by downtrodden peasants, and until at least the 1860s the native Catholic Irish were desperately poor and uneducated. Moreover, aspiring nationalism has nearly always been associated with liberal ideas, and the Irish Catholic Church has been particularly anti-liberal. When nationalists in other European countries were applauding the unification of Italy, Irish Catholics condemned Garibaldi as 'anti-Christ' and sent a contingent of volunteers to help defend the Vatican. It was not until the 1880s that the Catholic hierarchy supported a movement for Irish Home Rule.

The other unusual feature is that Ireland is the home not of one nationalist movement but of two. Ulster nationalism has excited far less interest in the outside world than Irish nationalism and has been inadequately understood. But because it is essentially a possessive nationalism rather than an aspiring nationalism it has been very effective in mobilising mass support: as Ireland's greatest political theorist indicated, people are usually readier to fight for an established right than for a speculative right.

The Growth of Irish Nationalism

When people are poverty-stricken, illiterate, and lack political resources, very few forms of political action are open to them. They can withhold rents, go on strike, and 'boycott' members of the ruling class (an Irish contribution to political tactics named after Captain Boycott, an Anglo-Irish landlord whose life was made intolerable by the refusal of his tenants and neighbours to speak to him, work for him or deal with him). They can also stage riots and demonstrations and engage in various acts of arson and violence. Britain's African colonies saw all these tactics before representative institutions were established, and so did Ireland. Rural lawlessness was a feature of Irish life throughout most of the eighteenth century and much of the nineteenth century.

But Irish nationalism, in the sense of a movement for Irish independence based on a sense of national identity, did not develop until the latter part of the nineteenth century. In the early years of the century the Irish Catholics found a leader in the person of Daniel O'Connell, but from 1807 till 1829 his main object was Catholic emancipation, i.e. the right of Catholics to sit in the UK Parliament and to hold government appointments. When this was granted he campaigned for various reforms and intermittently demanded the re-establishment of an Irish Parliament, though without compromising his allegiance to the Crown. This last demand gained only sporadic support and O'Connell certainly did not succeed in uniting the Irish people. He had 'hoped to win over the Presbyterians of the north', who also had little influence in government, but his close alliance with the rural Catholic clergy 'alarmed and alienated' the Presbyterians, and in the 1830s the latter 'definitely ranged themselves beside the established church in defence of the Union' (Beckett (a), pp. 153–4).

The 1840s saw the appalling tragedy of the famine, and following this there was a widespread breakdown of law and order in the countryside. Between 1847 and 1857 Parliament passed twelve Coercion Acts giving the executive special powers and suspending the normal liberties of the subject. But this lawlessness sprung out of wretched conditions and cannot be regarded as a form of nationalist revolt. Engels, who visited Ireland in 1856, described the Irish as 'utterly demoralised', unable to compete with the English and driven to the function 'of supplying England, America, Australia, etc. with prostitutes, casual labourers, pimps, thieves, swindlers, beggars and other rabble' (quoted Mansergh, p. 109). Cavour and Mazzini had also been there and both failed to find a movement that could truly be called nationalistic. Mazzini sympathised with Irish claims for better government but argued that they were not nationalist claims because the Irish 'did not plead for any distinct principle of life or system of legislation, derived from native peculiarities, and contrasting radically with English wants and wishes' (Mansergh, p. 96).

The genesis of Irish nationalism is to be found in three movements, one reformist, one revolutionary and one cultural, that developed in the latter part of the century. The reformist movement was the Home Rule League, founded by Isaac Butt in 1870, which captured 59 seats in the 1874 general election. The stated policy of the League was devolution within the United Kingdom, on quasi-federal lines, but the 1873 Home Rule Conference had asserted 'the inalienable right of the Irish people to self-government' and many of the speakers expressed themselves in favour of complete independence (Beckett (b), p. 382). Later in the seventies the cause of reform was taken up by the Land League, with Stewart Parnell as president, which constantly brought Irish problems to the attention of the Westminster Parliament. A number of legislative reforms were enacted, culminating in Wyndham's Land Act of 1903 which provided government financial aid for the wholesale transfer of farms and estates to the ownership of their tenants and finally ended the agrarian conflict which had plagued Ireland for generations.

The revolutionary movement was the Irish Republican Brotherhood (IRB), formed in 1858 as the consequence of plans made by embittered Irish exiles in Paris and (more important) New York. The IRB was a secret society whose members were bound by oath to terminate British rule in Ireland by force. Its members, generally known as Fenians, staged an abortive uprising in Ireland in March 1867, killed a policeman in Manchester in September, and killed twelve Londoners in December by setting off a bomb outside Clerkenwell prison (where one of their members was awaiting trial). Three Fenians were executed for the Manchester murder and have been known ever since in Ireland as 'the Manchester martyrs'.

The movement for the revival of Irish culture took several forms. In 1884 the Gaelic Athletic Association was established to encourage the traditional Irish sports of Gaelic football and hurling. It quickly became popular in the rural areas and acquired 50,000 members within a few years. The spirit of this Association was explicitly anti-English, and when it became established its members were prohibited from playing or watching any English games, on pain of expulsion. (The ban remained until 1971).

The intellectual equivalent of this movement was the Gaelic League, founded in 1893 to promote the use of the Gaelic language, with the ultimate aim of restoring it as the first language of the Irish nation. Patrick Pearse said in 1913 that the establishment of this League was 'the beginning of the Irish revolution' (see Paor, p. 64). The same decade saw a marvellous flowering of Irish literature – with George Moore, J. M. Synge,

W. B. Yeats and George Russell the leading figures – and while this literature was in English rather than Gaelic it nevertheless made a great contribution to the growth of national pride.

It is important not to under-estimate the significance of these cultural developments. If a nationalist movement is to take hold among a people, it needs both a visible enemy which can be blamed for the nation's problems and a positive sense of national identity, achievement and pride. For over 200 years the Irish had had a visible enemy, but until the last years of the nineteenth century they had lacked any evident basis for pride. Their history had been a long series of defeats and disasters, yielding few symbols of attachment except a haunting but melancholy set of folk-songs.

> Our prayers and our tears they have scoffed and derided,
> They've shut out God's sunlight from spirit and mind,
> Our foes were united and we were divided,
> We met and they scattered our ranks to the wind.

There is not much hope or inspiration in that ballad, or in this:

> We knelt at Mass with sobbing heart
>   Cold, in the dawn of day,
> The dawn for us, for him the night,
>   Who was so young and gay.
>
> Then from the Altar spoke the priest,
>   His voice rang thin with pain –
> Bidding us pray, a boy must die
>   At England's hands again.

Or in this:

> The battle it was over and the morn was shining bright;
> The stars shone o'er the dying and the dead,
> Not a sound was to be heard but the cry of the wild bird
> As it fluttered o'er a dying rebel's head.
> He whispered goodbye to his comrades so dear,
> His head upon his knapsack gently lay.
> 'If you ever see my home
> Tell my mother I'm alone,
> And I'm buried in an Irish rebel's grave.'

There are scores of ballads on the same general theme. 'The Wearing of the Green' is too well known to need repetition here, moving and significant though it is. But it is worth quoting from two songs which add a touch of self-recrimination to the pervasive air of sadness and defeat.

> But the gold sun of freedom grew darkened at Ross,
> And it set by the Slaney's red waves;
> And poor Wexford, stripped naked, hung high on a cross,
> And her heart pierced by traitors and slaves.

And, marginally less depressing:

> My curse upon all drinking! It made our hearts full sore;
> For bravery won each battle, but drink lost ever more.
> And if, for want of leaders, we lost at Vinegar Hill,
> We're ready for another fight, and love our country still.

The melancholy and sense of defeat in all these songs reflect the sadness of Irish history, and because of this the cultural developments at the end of the nineteenth century made a greater difference to Irish national consciousness than similar developments might have done elsewhere. Quite suddenly, Dublin attracted international attention as one of the cultural centres of the world, and for the first time the Irish realised they had something to feel proud of.

This new sense of national self-respect contributed to the foundation in 1905 of a new political movement called Sinn Fein, which can be translated as 'We Ourselves', 'Ourselves Alone', or simply 'Ourselves'. Its policy was the establishment of an Irish state completely independent of Britain, except that the two countries might share the same monarch, and it was proposed that Irish MPs should boycott the Westminster Parliament and meet in Dublin instead. Its founder was Arthur Griffith, an IRB member, but it enlisted the support not only of Fenians but also of well-known literary figures and an appreciable number of the country's other genuine or aspiring intellectuals. It did not attract wide support before 1914, for most Irish hopes were pinned to the prospect of achieving Home Rule by parliamentary means, but when these hopes were dashed it was this new separatist movement to which many Irish nationalists turned. (For an excellent short account of the origins and early days of Sinn Fein, see Kee, pp. 440–60).

Revolutionary Nationalism
Between 1912 and 1919 the politicians who had been campaigning for Irish Home Rule were swept aside by militant nationalists who led the country into armed conflict with the British authori-

ties. One reason for this was the development of Sinn Fein and the revival of IRB activities in Dublin. After 1907 the IRB was reinforced by the return of Tom Clarke, following fifteen years in English prisons, and the recruitment of a new group of dedicated young leaders like Patrick Pearse.

The second factor was the failure of the 1912 Home Rule Bill as a consequence of Ulster Protestant resistance. The British Liberals had not got much credit in Ireland for their espousal of Home Rule because, although Gladstone and some others were apparently sincere in their beliefs, the timing of their actions made them look like tactical manoeuvres. Liberal leaders made no attempt to introduce Home Rule when their party had a large majority in the Parliament of 1906–10 and only did so when they were dependent on Irish support after the 1910 elections. Their commitment to the cause was therefore suspect in Irish eyes, and the events of 1912–14 made many Irishmen despair of British politicians.

The strength of Ulster Protestant objections to Home Rule surprised nationalist leaders, who tended to blame the British for it. It was believed that the Protestants would not be threatening outright resistance to the measure without British encouragement, and this belief was strengthened when the leader of the Conservative and Unionist Party made it clear that the Protestants would have his support in their plans for disaffection: 'I can imagine no lengths to which Ulster Unionists might go where the Unionist Party and the public at large would not follow them in sympathy' (Bonar Law, 27 July 1912). The belief was further strengthened when British supporters sent supplies of money and arms to Ulster and when fifty-eight British cavalry officers stationed in Ireland declared their unwillingness to fight the Ulster Volunteers – a refusal that was accepted by the British authorities.

Many Irish nationalists have put this issue in a much broader perspective, viewing British policy in Ulster from the time of the original plantation as a plot to 'divide and rule' the Irish people. And while conspiracy theories of history are invariably misleading, British politicians over the years have made enough tactless remarks to lend some credence to this one, for those who wish to believe it. Liam de Paor's book *Divided Ulster* contains a moderate version of this theory which is particularly interesting because of his scholarly treatment of the matter.

The proposal to partition Ireland filled Irish nationalists with disgust. They viewed the Ulster Protestants as settlers who could be accepted as Irishmen if they wished to be; who would have the same constitutional rights as any other citizen; and who were absurdly misguided in their belief that a united Ireland would somehow be ruled by the Vatican. But IRB leaders predicted that the British Government would give way to the Protestants' threat of violence and drew the conclusion that the nationalists must take up arms also. Pearse put the matter as follows:

> It is foolish of an Orangeman to believe that his personal liberty is threatened by Home Rule; but, granting that he believes that . . . it is his clear duty to arm in defence of his threatened liberty. Personally I think the Orangeman with a rifle a much less ridiculous figure than the Nationalist without a rifle. (In *Irish Freedom*, November 1913, quoted in Paor, p. 72.)

The real split in the ranks of the nationalists occurred at the outbreak of the war with Germany. Redmond, the leader of the Home Rule party, pledged his support to the British government and urged Irishmen to join the British Army. Large numbers accepted this view and over 80,000 joined up. However, Pearse and the IRB saw the war as an opportunity to break with Britain while she was otherwise engaged and the socialist leader James Connolly and his tiny Citizen Army took the same view. It was these groups who organised the Easter Rising of 1916.

The Rising was of course a political gesture rather than an insurrection which had any serious chance of success. It was not even popular with Irish opinion:

> Never in the history of Ireland had a rebellion inspired so little sympathy. There were nearly 100,000 Catholic Irishmen fighting with the British Army, and the rebellion seemed as much a stab in the back to the majority of Irish people as it did to the English. The prisoners, who were marched through the streets, passed between lines of angry, jeering Dubliners. (Bennett, p. 9. See also Kee, p. 7.)

Opinion quickly changed, however, when fifteen of the sixteen rebel leaders were shot. This was a natural action for the authorities to take, since the leaders were clearly guilty of both treason and murder and the death penalty applied to both crimes. But it nevertheless proved to be the 'eruptive factor' which generated widespread support for the revolutionary movement. The Irish are a romantic people and

Almost overnight men whose names were unknown to most Irishmen became glorious martyrs in the national cause. . . . Ballads were composed in their honour. Yeats wrote 'a terrible beauty is born'. Postcard photographs of *The Men Who Died* decorated thousands of homes all over the country, so that when the prisoners were released in 1917 they returned to a hero's welcome. (Bennett, p. 10.)

The political value of martyrs was well understood by Pearse, who must have known he was signing his own death warrant when he took a leading role in the Easter Rising. Sometime earlier, he had expressed himself on the subject as follows:

The defenders of this Realm . . . think that they have pacified Ireland. They think that they have purchased half of us and intimidated the other half. They think that they have provided against everything: but the fools, the fools, the fools! – they have left us our Fenian dead, and while Ireland holds these graves, Ireland unfree shall never be at peace.

He had also written a poem entitled 'Renunciation', which ends with the following verse:

> I have turned my face
> To this road before me,
> To the deed that I see
> And the death I shall die.

Yeats understood the value of martyrs too, as he made clear in the last two verses of his poem on 'The Rose Tree' (of Irish nationalism):

> 'It needs to be but watered,'
> James Connolly replied,
> 'To make the green come out again
> And spread on every side,
> And shake the blossom from the bud
> To be the garden's pride'
>
> 'But where can we draw water,'
> Said Pearse to Connolly,
> 'When all the wells are parched away?
> O plain as plain can be,
> There's nothing but our own red blood
> Can make a right Rose Tree.'

In the following month Asquith, concerned that Ireland might become ungovernable, attempted to get the Home Rule Act implemented immediately. But this proved impossible, for British and Irish attitudes were both hardening in the aftermath of the Rising. In four successive by-elections members of the Home Rule party were defeated by Sinn Fein candidates, who then refused to take their seats. In October 1917 Sinn Fein agreed on the object of securing international recognition of Ireland as an independent Irish Republic, and Eamonn de Valera (who had drafted the resolution) became the official leader of the movement. De Valera was the sixteenth leader of the Rising, who had been sentenced to death but then reprieved, and quickly released, to placate American opinion, since he had been born in New York.

In April 1918 the government decided to extend conscription to Ireland. This was understandable, as the losses on the Western Front had been so catastrophic that the conscription age had to be raised to fifty, and the British public could not understand why one part of the kingdom should be exempt from the sacrifice. It was nevertheless an error of judgement which caused bitter resentment in Ireland and for the first time brought the Catholic hierarchy into open opposition to authority, the bishops issuing a statement which described the Conscription Act as 'an oppressive and inhuman law, which the Irish people had a right to resist by all the means that are consonant with the law of God'. An article was published urging nationalists to regard conscription as an act of war:

> We must recognise that anyone, civilian or soldier, who assists directly or by connivance in this crime against us, merits no more consideration than a wild beast, and should be killed without mercy or hesitation as opportunity offers. . . . Thus the man who serves on an exemption tribunal, the doctor who treats soldiers or examines conscripts, the man who voluntarily surrenders when called for, the man who in any shape or form applies for an exemption, the man who drives a police car or assists in the transport of army supplies, all these having assisted the enemy must be shot or otherwise destroyed with the least possible delay. (Quoted in Lyons, pp. 397–8.)

This is notable not only because its 'mood of cold savagery' (Lyons' term) indicates the hardening of attitudes since the Easter Rising but also because it is the earliest expression of the brutal philosophy which has motivated the Irish Republican

Army (IRA) from 1919 to the present day. In the event the Conscription Act was not implemented, so the revolutionaries benefited not only from the resentment its passage caused but also from this demonstration that the British authorities did not have the will to persist with an unpopular measure when faced with open threats of resistance.

In November 1918 the war ended, and the campaign by Sinn Fein and the IRA that followed the armistice was a textbook example of how to organise a nationalist revolution. The main object of any revolutionary group must be to erode the authority of the established government. In any society only a small minority of people are actively interested in politics and only a tiny minority are willing to risk their lives for a political cause. The overwhelming majority want to bring up their families and earn a living in peace, and are willing to acquiesce in the rule of whatever government provides a stable framework within which they can pursue their normal lives. They may not like the government of the day, but they accept the legitimacy of its rule.

The first crucial move by the revolutionary nationalists was to create confusion about legitimacy. In the general election of December 1918 Sinn Fein candidates swept the board in the Catholic areas of Ireland, winning 73 seats with 69 candidates (some of whom won more than one seat each). Instead of taking their seats in Parliament, these successful candidates met in Dublin and declared themselves the first Irish Assembly (or Dáil Eireann as it was called). With an eye on American opinion they issued a Declaration of Independence:

> Now, therefore, we, the elected Representatives of the ancient Irish people in National Parliament assembled do, in the name of the Irish nation, ratify the establishment of the Irish Republic and pledge ourselves and our people to make this Declaration effective by every means at our command.

The Dáil also appointed a government and the new ministers, though having to work in secret, nevertheless published statements of policy and in some cases were able to raise money. In most counties Sinn Fein established 'arbitration courts', with Republican Police (also operating in secret) to enforce their orders, and early in 1920 the party won control of the majority of local councils, which broke off relations with the Local Government Board. The ordinary citizen was therefore faced with two systems of government, one open but controlled by the British, the other underground but controlled by Irish nationalists.

The second crucial step was to undermine the morale of the Royal Irish Constabulary. This was done first by the time-honoured Irish method of boycotting and ostracising them, then by threatening them with assassination, and then by carrying out the threats. The morale of the force quickly weakened; there were many resignations; and it became impossible to attract Irish recruits. The Constabulary had to be strengthened with British volunteers, whose legitimacy in the eyes of citizens was weakened not only by their nationality and accents but also by the fact that, because of a shortage of police uniforms, they had to be dressed partly in British Army uniforms with black police belts. They were promptly christened the 'Black and Tans' (after a famous pack of hounds in Limerick).

It was not so easy to demoralise the Black and Tans, for they were a tough lot, hardened by trench warfare, who had come to Ireland to get away from the dole queues in British industrial cities. However, it proved fairly easy to discredit them by provoking them into retaliation and then waging a propaganda campaign against their behaviour. The pattern to be followed was set by the first serious case of retaliation, which involved troops rather than police. In September 1919 a party of English soldiers on their way to church parade in the small town of Fermoy were ambushed by an IRA unit in civilian clothes, who killed one soldier and wounded four others. At the inquest the following day the coroner praised the ambush as an act of warfare and the jury refused to bring in a verdict of murder. That evening a large body of soldiers smashed up the shops belonging to the jurors and some of their neighbours, causing damage valued at £3,000 (Bennett, p. 16).

The Black and Tans were less disciplined than the regular troops and their reprisals against IRA attacks were more vigorous and more bloody. The essence of what is sometimes called a war was in fact a series of assassinations, armed robberies and attacks on government buildings by IRA guerillas, followed by reprisal raids by the police (of whom about half, by 1922, were Black and Tans). The undisciplined nature of the reprisals, which included looting, arson and murder, upset public opinion in Britain. The Labour Party were more concerned about the reprisals than about the IRA, and both Arthur Henderson and Wedgwood Benn moved parliamentary resolutions attacking the government. Vocal opinion in America sympathised with the Irish nationalists, and Anglo-American relations were put under some strain. Lord Grey told the House of Lords that 'Ireland is a greater obstacle to international goodwill than any other question'. Without doubt, the revolutionaries won the war of propaganda.

If the British government had been willing to wage war in Ireland the struggle would of course have been one-sided. The IRA is said not to have had more than 15,000 men under arms and not more than 5,000 – or perhaps only 3,000 – on active service at any one time (Lyons, pp. 416–17). But the British never even contemplated a real war with Ireland. The Irish people were British citizens and the function of the armed forces is to defend British citizens, not attack them. The forces may come to the aid of the civil authorities in times of emergency, but it is a long-standing and firm British tradition that the role of the Army in times of civil disorder should be a strictly limited one of giving support to the police.

In any case, the British government had no real will to stay in the southern counties of Ireland. The Prime Minister had supported Home Rule since before the 1912 Bill and the Conservatives who made up the greater part of the ruling coalition were willing to wash their hands of the southern counties when they became an embarrassment. What they were totally unwilling to do was to capitulate to a gang of murderers (as they saw the IRA) and hand over the whole country on the latter's terms. The thought that they might conceivably do this, which delayed the peace treaty for months, indicates that the often-remarked inability of British politicians to understand the Irish was equalled on this occasion by the inability of Irish Republicans to understand the British. Gandhi and Nehru had more insight into the British mind than de Valera ever showed.

The peace treaty that was eventually signed gave the Irish Free State political independence, though with three conditions on which the British insisted. The first was the exclusion of six of the nine counties of Ulster, which remained part of the United Kingdom. The second was the maintenance of British bases in four Irish ports, to defend the Atlantic sea-routes in case of another European war. The third was that the Free State should remain part of the British Commonwealth, owing nominal allegiance to the Crown. In essence, it was a great victory for the nationalists, achieved with only a moderate cost in human lives. In round figures, 1,250 people were killed in nineteen months of insurrection, comprising 550 police and troops (mainly police), about 350 IRA men, and about 350 civilians (shot by both sides) (Bennett, pp. 166–7). But not everyone regarded it as a victory, and it left a residue of bitterness in Ireland that has not yet evaporated.

Ulster Nationalism

This term refers to the nationalistic beliefs and feelings of the Protestant community of the six north-eastern counties of Ireland which now constitute the Province of Northern Ireland. There is a certain geographical inaccuracy about this usage, as the medieval province of Ulster included not only these six counties but also three predominantly Catholic counties which are now in the Republic. But Northern Ireland is commonly referred to as Ulster and its Protestant citizens commonly describe themselves as Ulstermen. Its Catholic citizens never describe themselves in this way, but only as Irish.

There are two vital differences between Ulster nationalism and Irish nationalism. The first is that whereas Irish nationalism has always been based on ethnicity and place of birth, Ulster nationalism has always been based mainly on religion. Outside commentators have tended to regard the conflict between the two as being either a straightforward conflict between Catholics and Protestants or a straightforward conflict between natives and settlers. I do not believe that either of these interpretations is correct. One of the complications of the Irish situation is that the two forms of nationalism are different in character.

Irish nationalists always conceived of the struggle as being one between the people of Ireland and the British imperialists, and have been perfectly willing to accept non-Catholics as comrades or leaders. Parnell, the leader of the Irish Party, was a Protestant, as were Erskine Childers (secretary of the Irish delegation that negotiated the Peace Treaty of 1921) and Roger Casement (one of the leaders of the Irish Volunteers). James Connolly was a socialist of neo-Marxist convictions. Irish nationalists do not regard Ulstermen as foreign settlers but as Irishmen who have perversely rejected their natural place in the Irish nation. (Under the Constitution of the Irish Republic, which does not recognise the legitimacy of partition, all citizens of Northern Ireland are in fact entitled to claim Irish citizenship.)

Ulster nationalism, on the other hand, is essentially based on religion. All Ulster nationalists are Protestants and the ideology of the movement is strongly anti-Catholic. Because Ulstermen often call themselves Loyalists, some British commentators have regarded them as being more British than Irish. But this also is a mistake. Ulstermen see themselves as Irish with two distinctive qualities that mark them out from other Irishmen: (1) they are Protestants and have all the advantages and virtues that go with this; (2) they are loyal to the Union and the Crown whereas Catholics were or are disloyal.

The other difference between the two forms of nationalism in Ireland is that, whereas Irish nationalism was (until 1921) aspiring in character, Ulster nationalism has always been possessive in character. As indicated in Chapter 3, possessive nationalism tends to be stronger and more widespread than aspiring nationalism and this partly accounts for the rock-like qualities of Ulster nationalism.

The origins of Ulster nationalism clearly lie in the seventeenth century. In the words of one writer (reflecting the Irish sense of history that so mystifies the English), whereas Irish nationalists are constantly 'harping . . . back to the Gaelic past, real or imaginary', the mythology of Ulstermen 'is firmly anchored in the seventeenth century' (Fitzgibbon, p. 243). The events of that century were exceedingly dramatic and unpleasant. By 1641 about six-sevenths of the land of Ulster had been acquired by settlers from Scotland and England, although they constituted only a small proportion of the population. In the Ulster Rising of 1641 these settlers were attacked and slaughtered by the native Irish, in so far as they could not gain refuge in Protestant enclaves and forts. When Cromwell and his army arrived in 1649 they were appalled by what they found, and it has been said that Cromwell 'regarded the Irish whom he conquered as little better than dangerous wild beasts, to be exterminated' (Fitzgibbon, p. 34). His revenge on the Irish Catholics is remembered to this day, and it included the forced movement of many Catholics out of Ulster.

In 1689 the conflict was renewed on a wider scale, and this time the Ulster Protestants were able to defend themselves much more effectively. They held Londonderry, although greatly outnumbered, until an English relief force arrived by sea, and in the Battle of the Boyne they played a leading part in the defeat of James's army. The consequence was that, while the Ulster Rising had led them to despise and hate the Catholics, the battles of 1689–90 filled them with pride. For the next two centuries the Protestants dominated Ireland, not only politically but also socially and economically. And while the southern counties were wretchedly poor and affected by widespread lawlessness, Ulster was better off and more secure. Its economic superiority was noted by Continental visitors like de Tocqueville and de Beaumont (see Mansergh, ch. 1) as well as by English observers. And while Catholics tended to ascribe this to Protestant domination, the Ulstermen tended to credit it to their greater industry, more methodical farming methods, and membership of a church that encouraged thrift and self-reliance.

A clear statement of the Ulster Protestants' attitude was given in 1914 by J. B. Woodburn. After discussing and discounting race, climate, and history as reasons for the evident superiority of the North of Ireland over the South, he concluded that the chief reason for the difference was religion:

> The religion of the North is one that inculcates freedom of life and conscience, and must produce a more robust race of men than the South with its traditional and enervating Catholicism. Take the words of the calm, philosophical and judicious historian, Lecky, who speaks of Catholicism as follows – 'It is on the whole a lower type of religion than Protestantism, and it is peculiarly unsuited to a nation struggling with great difficulties. It is exceedingly unfavourable to independence of intellect and to independence of character, which are the first conditions of national progress. It softens, but it also weakens the character, and it produces habits of thought and life not favourable to industrial activity, and extremely opposed to political freedom.' (Woodburn, pp. 399–400.)

This Protestant feeling of superiority has continued right up to the present. A social anthropologist who did her field work in rural Ulster in the 1950s and early 1960s has reported that:

> While Ulster Catholics tended to ascribe their . . . poverty to the machinations of the Protestants, the latter believed it to be the inevitable consequence of the Catholics' adherence to a church that imposed heavy financial burdens on its members, prevented them from limiting their families sensibly, and sought to keep them docile through ignorance. (Harris, p. 177.)

The contempt with which the Ulster Protestants have regarded the Irish Catholics was of course greatly increased by the evidence of Catholic lawlessness and disloyalty. The Fenian bombings of 1867 outraged the Protestants; the support of Irish nationalists for the Boers in the Boer War – and some nationalists went to fight on the Boer side – was regarded by the Protestants as treason; the Easter Rising and the resistance to conscription during the First World War were regarded as matters of shame – to say nothing of the attempt to raise an Irish Brigade from among prisoners-of-war in Germany which would fight on the German side. Eight Protestant leaders sent an open letter to Woodrow Wilson on 1 August 1918 in which they said that they had 'maintained throughout the present war that the same obligations should in all respects be borne by Ireland as by Great Britain, and it has caused them as Irishmen a keen sense of shame that their country has not submitted to this equality of sacrifice'. Moreover, the Protestant leaders laid part of the blame on the shoulders of the Catholic Church:

> The most active opponents of conscription in Ireland are men who have been twice detected during the war in treasonable traffic with the enemy, and their most powerful support has been that of ecclesiastics, who have not scrupled to employ weapons of spiritual terrorism which have elsewhere in the civilized world fallen out of political use since the Middle Ages. (See McNeill, app. B.)

Fifty years later, some of these feelings were neatly encapsulated in the 'provocative slogan' which a small group of Ulster policemen used when hammering on the doors of Catholic houses after two days of rioting in Londonderry in 1969. The slogan was: 'Come on out you Fenian bastards and we'll give you one for the Pope' (Cameron Report, para. 177).

The essential conditions for the development of Ulster nationalism therefore existed sometime before the emergence of Irish nationalism as an effective force. On the positive side, the Protestants had a tight sense of communal unity combined with strong feelings of pride in their achievements. They did not have to wait for a literary movement to give them this sense, as they derived it partly from their military victories over the Catholics in the late seventeenth century and partly from their economic superiority. These feelings of pride and solidarity were enhanced by the activities of the Orange Order (a nationalist organisation founded in 1795), which organised between five and eight hundred marches each year to commemorate past victories and reaffirm present loyalties until these marches were curtailed by the violence which began in 1969. Since there are only one million Ulster Protestants this represents a high level of nationalist activity. On the negative side the Protestants had a clear enemy of whose presence they were continually aware, who heavily outnumbered them until the partition, but who were thought inferior in all other respects.

Since the Protestants dominated Ireland from 1689 onwards, their nationalism gained strength from its possessive character. When Gladstone's conversion to Home Rule was announced in 1885, this produced a strong and immediate reaction from the Protestants which could have been predicted by anyone with a clear understanding of Irish politics (a category which did not include Gladstone or many of his Liberal colleagues). Indeed, sixteen days before the announcement of this conversion burst like a bombshell on the English political scene, the Orange Order leader, William Johnson, had given the following warning in a public speech in Dublin:

> The day that any Government brings into the House of Commons a Bill to separate Ireland from England . . . the Orange Volunteers would be mustered in Ireland under able and experienced officers, and if the Bill proceeded further and received the Royal Assent there would be at once a civil war in Ulster. (See Kee, p. 400.)

Randolph Churchill was one of the very few British politicians who knew Ireland (having lived in Dublin when his father was Governor-General), and his famous remark in 1886 – 'Ulster will fight and Ulster will be right' – was based on a genuine understanding of the Irish dilemma as well as being a ploy to advance his own career in the Conservative Party by leading the attack on Gladstone. It is noteworthy that when the 1912 Home Rule Bill was drafted Randolph's son Winston wanted to exclude Ulster from its terms, but got no support from any of his colleagues in the Liberal Cabinet apart from Lloyd George.

The political position of the Ulster nationalists from 1885 onwards was quite straightforward. Since the extensions of the franchise in 1867 and 1884 an all-Irish Parliament would inevitably be dominated by Catholics; the Protestants believed that the Catholics would not rest until they had turned Home Rule into independence; and they were totally unwilling to be put into a situation in which they would be at the mercy of their historic enemies. The strength of the Orange Order was greatly increased by the first Home Rule Bill, and other organisations, such as the Ulster Loyalist and Patriotic Union, were formed to espouse the same cause. The second Home Rule Bill of 1893 further strengthened the resolve of Ulster nationalists to defend their position by any means found necessary, and in the 1890s 'arms were being illegally imported, rifle clubs were springing up everywhere, and sextons of church halls were moulding bullets in their furnaces' (Stewart, p. 32). In 1907 the secretary of the Belfast Reform Club placed advertisements in several Continental newspapers asking for 10,000 rifles (McNeill, p. 191).

Notwithstanding this clear evidence of the determination of Ulster nationalists, the Liberal Government was apparently surprised by the strength of the objections to the third Home Rule Bill of 1912. Asquith and most of his colleagues showed themselves to be as incapable of understanding the Ulster nationalists as they were of understanding the leaders of the Easter Rising four years later. The 1912 Bill provoked passionate controversy in Britain also, partly because it resulted from a secret bargain between Asquith and Redmond (leader of the Irish Party) whereby the latter had promised to support the Liberals in their various other policies in return for Home Rule. The Liberals had carefully avoided mentioning Home Rule during their two election campaigns of 1910, and the Conservatives were therefore able to claim that it was illegitimate for the government (which had not even secured a clear majority in the House of Commons) to push through a major constitutional reform for which they had no mandate. This was one of the reasons why the Conservatives supported the Ulster nationalists in their plans to prevent the implementation of the reform by any means, including civil war if this proved necessary.

The events following the introduction of the 1912 Home Rule Bill are well known and need only the briefest of outlines. The Ulster Unionists chose as their leader Sir Edward Carson, a barrister of outstanding brilliance who came from Dublin and was dedicated to the maintenance of the union of Ireland and England. They organised a petition against the Bill which was signed by 490,000 Ulster Protestants. They formed the Ulster Volunteer Force to serve as their army in case of need, imported between 30,000 and 40,000 rifles and several million rounds of ammunition in a single operation, and made detailed plans to establish a Provisional Government of Ulster. Their sympathisers in Britain, led by Lord Milner, collected nearly 2 million signatures to a British Covenant which read:

> I . . . . . of . . . . . earnestly convinced that the claim of the Government to carry the Home Rule Bill into law without submitting it to the judgment of the Nation is contrary to the spirit of our Constitution, do hereby solemnly declare that if that Bill is passed I shall hold myself justified in taking or supporting any action that may be effective to prevent it being put into operation, and more particularly to prevent the armed forces of the Crown being used to deprive the people of Ulster of their rights as citizens of the United Kingdom. (Quoted in Riddell, p. 19.)

One of the constant themes of Ulster nationalist propaganda was that their long-standing loyalty to the Union was being betrayed by the British Government in a political manoeuvre to gain short-term party advantage for the Liberals. In one of his speeches in Belfast, Carson asked:

> Is our reward to be that we are to be turned outside the United Kingdom; that we are to be put in a degraded position in the Empire; and above all that we are to be handed over, bound hand and foot, to those who have ever been Your Majesty's enemies and ours? (Quoted in T. D. Williams, p. 91.)

Similar sentiments were expressed in a poem by William Watson entitled 'Ulster's Reward', which was published in *The Times* – of less literary merit than much Irish nationalist poetry, but nevertheless conveying its message more forcefully than prose.

> What is the wage the faithful earn?
> What is a recompense fair and meet?
> Trample their fealty under your feet -
> That is a fitting and just return.
>> Flout them, buffet them, over them ride,
>> Fling them aside!
>
> Ulster is ours to mock and spurn,
> Ours to spit upon, ours to deride.
> And let it be known and blazoned wide
> That this is the wage the faithful earn:
>> Did she uphold us when others defied?
>> Then fling her aside.
>
> Where on the Earth was the like of it done
> In the gaze of the sun?
> She had pleaded and prayed to be counted still
> As one of our household through good and ill,
>> And with scorn they replied;
> Jeered at her loyalty, trod on her pride,
>> Spurned her, repulsed her,
>> Great-hearted Ulster;
> Flung her aside.

With a nationalist movement of this strength and conviction facing the Irish nationalist movement described above, there could only be one outcome to the move towards Home Rule, namely the partition of Ireland. If Asquith and his colleagues had not been so ignorant, complacent and anxious for party advantage, they might have accepted this from the outset, and thus saved much agony and possibly a good deal of bloodshed.

As it was, the partition was delayed until 1921, was based on existing county boundaries instead of on rational criteria, and created a Province of Northern Ireland with a large Catholic minority comprising 35 per cent of the population.

Relations between the communities had naturally deteriorated during the years of fighting and the new Province was launched with a minority who disputed its legitimacy and a majority made even more determined to safeguard their interests by the feeling that they could place little trust in the British government and the fear that the higher birthrate among the Catholics might eventually give them a majority of the electorate. This latter fear has proved unjustified, as the higher Catholic birthrate has been exactly balanced by higher emigration and the relative sizes of the two communities have remained constant. But the fear affected Protestant attitudes for some time.

Since partition, the character of Ulster nationalism has hardly changed. The Ulstermen's feelings of communal pride have been reinforced by the considerable contribution they made to the Allied cause in the Second World War, when their ports were invaluable bases for the defence of the Atlantic sea-routes and, though not conscripted, they volunteered in large numbers and provided the three most successful generals of the British Army (Lords Alanbrooke, Alexander and Montgomery). Their negative feelings towards Irish Catholics have been reinforced by the policies of the Roman Catholic Church, by the activities of the IRA, by the refusal of the Republic to extradite IRA men charged with murder, and by the neutral stance of the Republic during the war. They despised the Republic for refusing to allow their ports to be used for the defence of the sea-routes and for their studied policy of neutrality, which went so far as to include a telegram of condolence from de Valera to the German government when Hitler's death was announced. Their suspicions of Britain have been revived by events since 1969, which will be discussed in the following chapter. Suffice it to say here that they have good reason to believe that the English have little understanding of their problems and little regard for their loyalty. As one Ulsterman has recently observed:

The responses of the present-day English as a whole to events in Ireland declare an ignorance and a superior disapproval which make the well-read Irishman wince. (Riddell, p. ix.)

5
Ireland: Disintegration and Its Lessons

The events between 1912 and 1922 led to a partial disintegration of the United Kingdom. Twenty-six of Ireland's thirty-two counties formed an independent state and the remaining six constituted a province which remained within the United Kingdom, though with a considerable measure of devolution.

These events aroused passionate controversy and the arguments about them have not yet died away. But, half a century on, it is worth trying to make a dispassionate assessment of the costs and benefits of the operation and to see what lessons can be drawn from it that may be relevant to the problem of relationships between England, Wales and Scotland.

Such an assessment falls naturally into three parts. First, there is the cost of the method by which disintegration was brought about, a campaign of guerilla warfare which involved brutal acts by both sides. The price paid for this was widespread bitterness, civil war, and the continued existence of an underground army that claims to be the heir to the Republican tradition. Secondly, there is the progress of the Irish state since it achieved independence. At a time when politicians are arguing about the possible benefits of independence for Scotland and Wales, it is clearly relevant to ask how far Ireland has been able to achieve the cultural, political and economic goals that her leaders have prescribed. Thirdly, there is the question of how successful partition has been as a device for dealing with the conflicts within Irish society, which raises the political problems of Northern Ireland and the question of whether devolution is desirable if it leads to the creation of a regional assembly in which one party has a permanent majority.

Each of these three questions could well occupy a whole book and it is impossible to deal adequately with them in a brief summary. But they are so important to the subject of this book, and to current political controversies in the United Kingdom, that it is essential to examine them, even though only in outline.

THE REPUBLICAN TRADITION

> Park your car in the city of Dublin, see Sackville Street
> Without the sandbags in the old photos, meet
> The statues of the patriots, history never dies,
> At any rate in Ireland, arson and murder are legacies
> Like old rings hollow-eyed without their stones
> Dumb talismans.
>
> Louis MacNeice

In the 1922 settlement the Irish Free State was given the status of a self-governing member of the British Commonwealth, with a position virtually identical to that of Canada or Australia. To English observers, it is therefore difficult to understand why the settlement should have led to such a furious controversy among the Irish revolutionaries that they took up arms against each other and led their infant state into a bloody civil war. It is true that the six north-eastern counties were excluded from the Free State, but that was not the cause of the civil war. The long debate on the Treaty in the Dáil Eireann occupies 338 pages in the official report, of which only nine are devoted to partition (Wall, p. 87). The real focus of controversy was the Oath of Allegiance to be taken by Members of Parliament in the Free State, which stuck in the gullet of many Irish leaders even though the wording had been modified to meet Irish susceptibilities. Allegiance had, in fact, to be given primarily to the Constitution of the Free State and only secondarily to the Crown as Head of the Commonwealth:

I . . . . . . do solemnly swear true faith and allegiance to the Constitution of the Irish Free State as by law established and that I will be faithful to H.M. King George V, his heirs and successors by law, in virtue of the common citizenship of Ireland with Great Britain and her adherence to and membership of the group of nations forming the British Commonwealth of Nations.

Why were Irish leaders more upset about the symbolism of the Oath than about the reality of partition? The answer to this question falls into two parts. The first part is that for various reasons they were willing to accept partition as a temporary expedient to secure British withdrawal from the rest of Ireland. The IRA had done rather well in its fight against the Irish police and the Black and Tans, but it was weakened by the end of 1921 and was certainly in no condition to take on the new Special Constabulary of the Protestant north-east and the 40,000 or more armed men of the Ulster Volunteers. If Ulster could not be taken by force it was sensible to think of taking it by political means, and one concession had been gained which held out slight hopes of this. Lloyd George had promised a boundary commission to review the location of the border and many nationalists believed that this commission might reduce Northern Ireland to a fragment too small to be viable. This belief was illusory in two senses. It was illusory, first, because when it came to the point the Commission simply confirmed the existing border; and, secondly, because if the area of Northern Ireland had been reduced this action would probably have strengthened the Province politically rather than weakened it, by reducing the size of its Catholic minority. But the belief swayed opinion at the crucial time of decision.

The other half of the story is that most IRA leaders regarded the Free State as a constitutional step backwards rather than an advance. In their eyes they had not been fighting for British agreement to some kind of constitutional change which was to be negotiated. They had been fighting for British recognition of the Irish Republic that had been proclaimed on the steps of the Dublin Post Office at the beginning of the Easter Rising and confirmed by the first Dáil Eireann in 1918. To abandon the Republic would be a betrayal of their comrades who had died in the struggle. One IRA leader, Liam Lynch, said: 'We have declared for an Irish Republic and will not live under any other law.' Another, Cathal Brugha, declared in the Dáil: 'There is only one way the dastards responsible for disestablishing the Republic can ever extirpate this crime. And it is by dying for Ireland.' De Valera formed a new Republican Party (Cumann na Poblachta) and he said that if the fighters of the previous four years wanted to complete their work they 'would have to wade through Irish blood, through the blood of the soldiers of the Irish Government, and through perhaps the blood of some members of the Government, in order to get Irish freedom' (quoted in Holt, p. 287).

In June 1922 a general election was held in which pro-Treaty candidates won 92 seats and anti-Treaty candidates won 36. The Provisional Government regarded this result as constituting public endorsement of the Treaty, and their opponents reacted with violence. Six days after the election two members of the London battalion of the IRA assassinated Field-Marshal Sir

Henry Wilson (former Chief of the Imperial General Staff) in an attempt to upset relations between the Provisional Government and the British Government. Four days later the Assistant Chief of Staff of the Provisional Government's army was kidnapped and held captive in an IRA garrison in Dublin. On the following day Government forces began shelling this garrison and the civil war 'began in earnest' (Holt, p. 296).

The war lasted almost a year and was singularly unpleasant. It has often been said that revolutions devour their children and the Irish case proved to be no exception. The long list of Irish martyrs was swollen by the death of many of those who had led the revolt against British rule, this time at the hands of their former comrades. Whereas the British had executed 24 people in cold blood during the nineteen months of the revolt, the new Irish government executed 77 during the eleven months of civil war. Large numbers of civilians were killed and over 12,000 people were held in internment camps. At the end de Valera agreed to surrender and sent a message to his guerilla forces which said: 'Military victory must be allowed to rest with those who have destroyed the Republic.' The feelings of the Republicans have been summarised thus by the historian of the IRA:

The glorious dream of Easter 1916 had gone. There was to be no Republic. There was only to be a mean, bitter Ireland, partitioned by the Crown, governed by murderers imposed by the British. (Bell, pp. 54–5.)

It was in this way that Ireland became burdened with one of the most extraordinary underground armies the world has ever seen. All but one of its specific grievances have long since disappeared, since the Oath was abolished in 1933, the British abandoned the naval bases in 1938, and the Free State became the Republic of Ireland in 1949. But IRA members have never forgiven the British for their long colonisation of Ireland, the Ulster Protestants for forcing a partition in 1912–20, or the Dublin authorities for accepting the fruits of the compromise of 1921–2. No matter that the actual offenders are dead, for to Irishmen brought up in this tradition the passage of time does not so much heal the wounds of the past as turn them into myths to justify further sacrifices. Much blood has been shed for the Republican cause in previous generations, and those who accept the Republican mythology can only express their loyalty to the cause by shedding more blood. Sometimes this loyalty is pathetically personal, as when teenage girls engage in terrorist activities to avenge the death of their father or grandfather, uncle or great-uncle. But the Republicans are expert at exploiting emotions, and the gunman-become-martyr, often enshrined in a folk-song, is an effective way of both personalising the cause and ennobling what might otherwise be seen as a squalid and point-less death.

There are several other factors which have contributed to the success of this illegal organisation to survive for (so far) nearly sixty years. The continuance of partition, coupled with evidence of discrimination against Catholics in Northern Ireland, has kept a real issue alive which attracts supporters. The claim of the IRA that it functions as a 'home guard' for the Catholic ghettoes of Belfast and Londonderry earns sympathy for the Army from among many who would never think of joining it. The lack of extradition across the Irish border has made it easy for gunmen to commit raids in the North and secure sanctuary in the Republic. The support of Irish-American organisations has ensured a plentiful supply of money and arms from across the Atlantic. The success of the Army in intimidating witnesses and jurors has made it very difficult for the police to secure convic-tions against IRA members in the courts.

There was considerable continuity in IRA activities between 1923 and 1969. They organised both social clubs and bank robberies to secure funds; they imported arms from overseas; they trained and disciplined their men, using brutal methods to punish indiscipline; and from time to time they launched cam-paigns of violence in Northern Ireland. These campaigns damaged property, blew up police stations and electricity lines, killed policemen, and produced more martyrs for the cause. In 1957, for instance, an IRA unit tried to blow up a Royal Ulster Con-stabulary (RUC) barracks in Armagh with a land mine. The raid was a complete failure and two of the attackers, named South and O'Hanlon, were killed in an exchange of machine-gun fire.

> When the bodies of South and O'Hanlon were carried across the border, their transmutation from young men to martyrs began. . . . Crowds lined the route of South's funeral cortege to Dublin. Larger crowds came to pay their respect. Mass cards piled up and overflowed. Town Councils and County Corporations passed votes of sympathy. (Bell, p. 353.)

There must have been many citizens of the Republic who took an entirely different view of the incident, but this quotation illuminates the political atmosphere which has enabled the IRA to survive and prosper.

Occasionally the Army has also launched attacks on targets in England. In 1938 it decided to go to war with Britain, and arms and agents were carefully planted in English cities – the transportation presenting no serious problems as Irish citizens have always been treated as if they were British citizens and in normal times there are no border checks. In January 1939 an official ultimatum was delivered to the British Foreign Secretary threatening war within four days unless the British Government promised to withdraw from Northern Ireland. The ultimatum was completely ignored and on the fourth day electricity supplies were disrupted by seven explosions in different parts of England, from London to the Scottish border. The next twelve months saw a very large number of IRA bomb attacks in England. Bombs were exploded in post offices, electricity stations, banks, hotels, cinemas and Underground stations. On 31 May the police searched every cinema in London following explosions in two of them. In August 5 people were killed and 60 injured in a shopping centre in Coventry. But security measures became more and more effective as the months passed and the campaign had to be abandoned in January 1940. In 1974 and 1975 English cities again suffered from IRA bombs, some planted by agents sent across the water and others by 'sleepers', Irishmen who have been living normal lives in England until activated by an order. The extraordinary hold that the IRA maintains over its members was illustrated by the Birmingham bombings of November 1974, when 21 people were killed and 161 injured by explosions in two crowded pubs in the centre of the city. The six men found guilty of planting these bombs were all local residents, who had lived peacefully with their families in Birmingham for periods of between twelve and twenty-eight years, but were yet ready to murder a random group of fellow-residents (and risk life imprisonment themselves) for the sake of the Republican cause.

The IRA has, however, had one major success in recent years. In 1969 it took advantage of tension in Northern Ireland to start a campaign there which has induced the British Government to take measures which shattered the Ulster Unionist Party which had ruled the Province since 1920. Whether the Catholic minority in the North have benefited from this campaign is open to question. Hundreds of them have been killed or seriously wounded; hundreds more have been made homeless; the unemployment rate has increased; and the conditions of daily life have deteriorated, particularly in Belfast. But the Ulster Unionist ascendancy has been broken and the IRA undoubtedly regard the campaign as their greatest success since 1921.

There is one further aspect of the revolutionary tradition that deserves comment. Any organisation that engages in revolutionary activities has problems of security. Its members may be reported by neighbours and its branches infiltrated by police agents. Violent measures are needed to deal with spies and to intimidate possible informers. From the beginning the IRA has accepted this need. Between January and April 1921, 73 Irish men and women were murdered by the IRA and their bodies left by the roadside with a placard attached which read 'A warning to spies' (Holt, p. 241).

In subsequent years the IRA established court-martial proceedings (normally held in the absence of the accused person) and a range of punishments for disloyalty. Spies are shot through the back of the head; lesser offences are punished by bullets through the kneecaps or by tarring and feathering. These punishments are meted out constantly: between January 1974 and May 1975, for instance, there were 134 cases of IRA 'knee-capping' known to the Northern Ireland police (*Guardian*, 8 June 1975). The punishments extend to women as well as to men. In one case a pregnant woman in Belfast who was found guilty of some mild form of disloyalty was stripped naked, tied to a lamp-post, and had a tin of red paint poured over her head. She was left shivering there, while neighbours jeered, until a security patrol eventually cut her free.

Lest it be thought that these comments betray an English bias, I should like to quote from a letter to the Dublin *Irish Times* written by a resident of a Catholic housing estate in Belfast after a visit to the Republic.

We who live in the midst of the obscenity and are able to escape momentarily to the South for a break . . . are conscious of an air of unreality about the replies we get when we are forced into discussing our experiences. As we listen to the soft plámás in that Southern accent, and the half-hinted justification of terror, it is impossible not to return to the North with a feeling of disquiet.

But then not (yet?) for them the shot in the night and the cry of 'Oh, Mammy!' and venture out to find a sixteen-year-old boy knee-capped by a group of boys and girls; not for them to know personally a youth who pleaded for his life as he had 'dropped out a year ago' but was gunned down in front of his terrified workmates all the same; not for them to [hear a Sinn

Fein official on television] offering condolences to a man whose six-year-old daughter was murdered by bullets fired by its 'military wing' and intended for him ('we are sorry your child was murdered instead of you'). (*Irish Times*, 20 November 1975.)

This is a lasting feature of the republican tradition in Ireland. The price of this tradition is to be measured not only in terms of the lives it has cost but also in terms of the brutalisation of a section of the population, the intimidation of a much larger section, and the poisoning of the political and social life of whole communities. It is to be hoped that the English, the Welsh and the Scots will learn from this tragic story and manage their forthcoming conflicts without resort to violence.

The attitudes of the Irish authorities to the IRA have been somewhat ambivalent. Ever since 1932 Fianna Fáil has been the largest single party in the Irish Parliament and for most of this period it has formed a single-party government. Although Fianna Fáil leaders have been embarrassed by IRA activities, and the IRA is indeed an illegal organisation, the fact that Fianna Fáil was formed by men who had opposed the Treaty of 1921 meant that many of the party's supporters had a residual emotional sympathy with the IRA's history and aims. They might not approve of the continuation of the struggle but they recognised that it had once been their struggle, or their parents' struggle, and would therefore not have supported drastic measures by the authorities to crush the Army.

In recent years the authorities have become tougher, and it is now possible for IRA members to be sent to prison if they are identified by a police inspector in special courts, which operate without juries. However, this tough policy applies only to IRA members convicted of operating in the Republic and does not extend to those who operate in Northern Ireland or Great Britain. The latter are free to use the Republic as a sanctuary and are protected by the 1965 Extradition Act, which makes extradition impossible not only for political offences but also for 'offences related to political offences'. This means that persons wanted by the UK government for murder, arson or possessing explosives will not be extradited by Irish courts if they claim that their crimes were committed as part of an IRA campaign.

Between 1968 and 1976 the British authorities brought 56 cases of this kind before the Irish courts and extradition was refused on every occasion. In the case of fugitive offenders, IRA membership can therefore be a legal asset in a country where the

IRA is itself illegal. In 1975 a convict serving a term of imprisonment in Belfast for robbery with violence escaped from jail and found refuge in the Republic. When extradition was sought it was refused by the Irish court after the convict claimed that the robbery had in fact been committed to secure funds for the IRA.

It is difficult for the British public to regard the refusal of the Irish authorities to amend their extradition laws with understanding. But both press and people in Britain fail to understand the depth of anti-British feeling that still exists in Irish political circles, over fifty years after independence. In November 1975 the Government Chief Whip condemned the British press as 'disgraceful' for criticising his country's extradition laws, and went on to say:

> the kind of reaction lately visible in the British press might be venial if it had come from the press in Italy or in France, countries which never did Ireland any harm. . . . In the case of Britain, while no argument known to civilized man could possibly justify or extenuate the vile horrors committed there in the usurped name of Ireland . . . it is possible to push us into reminding these strident journalists that what is now being paid is the price of British indifference and neglect [in Northern Ireland] in the years before 1969. (*Irish Times,* 5 December 1975.)

In view of this attitude, it was not surprising that in November 1976 the Irish Government representatives in the Council of Europe refused to sign a convention listing terrorist-type crimes that should no longer be considered political offences in extradition cases between European states.

The best way to conclude this section is by quoting from the reflections of the president of the Welsh nationalist party, Plaid Cymru, on the Irish heritage of violence.

> In my view the history of Modern Ireland is a warning against resort to violence in the cause of national freedom. . . . If there were less Irishmen ready to live than to shoot and die for Ireland it was because of the uncritical Irish acceptance of the convention that violence is alone heroic and effective. This gave the men of violence and their methods a status that tended to overshadow the aims for which they fought. The continued glorification of violence in Ireland bedevils the situation north and south of the border; it is the soil in which

the IRA and UDA have grown so lushly. . . . Had it [Ireland] relied on nonviolent methods, it would have achieved more, if a few years later. (Evans (*b*), p. 16.)

THE PROGRESS OF THE NEW STATE

The achievements of the new state since 1922 can usefully be discussed under three headings: first, its success in achieving genuine political independence from the United Kingdom; secondly, its success in bringing about the revival of the Irish language which many Irish nationalists envisaged; and, thirdly, its success in achieving economic independence, promoting economic growth, and stemming the rate of emigration.

The Treaty of 1921 did not impose any significant limitations on the political independence of the new state. The Oath of Allegiance was only a formality and, although Ireland was given the British system of parliamentary and cabinet government, this was the system that the Irish would have chosen for themselves and which they continued in the new Constitution of 1937. The right of the Royal Navy to use four Irish ports was ceded by Neville Chamberlain in 1938, and when Britain went to war with Germany in 1939 Ireland not only proclaimed her neutrality but also refused to permit the use of these naval bases to guard the Western Approaches. Irish independence of the United Kingdom in the field of diplomacy has been amply demonstrated on numerous occasions.

In one respect, however, the first constitution which the Irish drafted entirely themselves, namely that of 1937, was markedly different from its predecessors. The 1937 Constitution contained several clauses which reflected the dominant position of the Roman Catholic Church in Ireland. Article 41 recognised the family as a 'moral institution possessing inalienable and imprescriptible rights, antecedent and superior to all positive law'. The enactment of laws establishing a right of divorce is forbidden and a person who has secured a divorce in another country is denied the right to remarry within Ireland if his original marriage is recognised in Irish law. Articles 42, 43, 44 and 45 are also based on Roman Catholic doctrines and recognise the special position of the Roman Catholic Church. These constitutional provisions did not imply any political discrimination against Protestants, one or two of whom achieved high positions in public life in the early years of the Republic. However, Protestants had to accept the fact that they lived in a society dominated by the Catholic Church, in which divorce was impossible, literature was subject to strict censorship on moral grounds, and the sale or importation of contraceptives was banned until the 1970s. It is therefore not surprising that many Protestants have moved out of the country, either to the North or to Britain. Extreme pressure by the Catholic Church, backed by legal sanctions, has also meant that the children of mixed marriages have generally been brought up as Catholics. As a result of these two factors the proportion of Protestants in the twenty-six counties has declined from 11 per cent in 1911 to 4 per cent in 1971. Needless to say, the special position of the Catholic Church in the Republic has also reinforced the determination of Ulster Protestants to oppose any suggestion of Irish unification.

The Irish Language

Irish nationalists believed that one of the benefits of independence would be the revival of the Irish language and a consequent revival of the traditional culture of rural Ireland. The new Provisional Government of 1922 lost no time in introducing compulsory teaching of Irish in all primary schools which had a competent teacher in the subject, and as the majority of teachers could not then speak Irish the Government also launched a crash programme of language courses for them. The 1922 Constitution made Irish the national language and, although English is also used, Irish has primacy in all official documents. It was decreed that civil servants, police and members of the armed forces should acquire some proficiency in it.

This policy has had only a limited success. Although the overwhelming majority of teachers are now capable of teaching Irish, and about 40 per cent of the time in primary schools is devoted to language instruction, the proportion of the population over the age of three claiming to be able to speak Irish rose only from 18·5 per cent in 1911 to 28·3 per cent in 1961. It has to be accepted that all the pressures of modern life militate against the revival of an essentially rural language of this kind. Only in a few rural enclaves, known collectively as the Gaeltacht, is the language spoken in normal conversation, and estimates of the number of people who actually use Irish as their first language vary from 35,000 to 60,000, that is, between 1 and 2 per cent of the population. Less than 2 per cent of the speeches in the Irish Parliament are given in Irish and its use by civil servants is negligible except in the Department of the Gaeltacht and, to a lesser extent, the Department of Education (Commission on the Restoration of the Irish Language, pp. 21–4).

The results of the campaign to revive the Irish language have therefore been disappointing. Irish is hardly spoken in the greater part of the country, and although it has survived in the Gaeltacht these Irish-speaking areas suffer from rural poverty and their population has greatly declined in the past fifty years. The government has made substantial efforts to prevent their decline, but the development of the tourist industry in the Gaeltacht, while alleviating their poverty, has also brought an influx of English-speaking visitors. It has been reported that the psychological impact of these affluent visitors has been to associate the Irish language 'with penury, drudgery and backwardness, and English, by contrast, with wealth, ease and advancement' (O Cuiv, p. 120). In 1972 a new Irish-speaking radio station was opened, beamed at the Gaeltacht and broadcasting for three hours each day, and other measures are canvassed by language enthusiasts. But the conclusion of the historian F. S. L. Lyons is that 'time is inexorably running out' and 'the future of the language . . . [is] balanced on a knife edge' (Lyons, p. 645). A professor of modern languages has predicted that the language 'will become moribund early in the next century and therefore extinct by the end of it' (Lockwood, p. 78).

To some extent the fate of the language remains a matter of controversy. Many educationalists have criticised the amount of time devoted to it in the schools, which does not lead children to use the language but does have an adverse effect on their proficiency in English (see Macnamara for details). The requirement that all students must pass in Irish to get their School Leaving Certificate has been dropped, as has the requirement that all recruits to the civil service must pass a language test.

Nevertheless, public opinion polls have always shown a majority to be in favour of the continuation of language teaching, as the language is still to some extent a symbol of Irish nationalism. It is given pride of place over English on road signs, with the convention that Irish directions are printed in italics and English ones in block capitals so as not to confuse motorists. It is possible that future generations of Irishmen will so take their nationhood for granted, and take pride in their membership of a prosperous modern state, that they will come to regard this symbol of national identity as superfluous. But that time has not yet been reached, and those who care about the maintenance of the language for cultural reasons will undoubtedly use the political argument in the attempt to preserve it.

Economic Independence

When Ireland became independent in 1922 her economy was almost entirely dependent upon that of Britain. Ninety-six per cent of Irish exports went to the UK and her essential function was to provide agricultural produce for the British market. Over 50 per cent of employed persons in Ireland were engaged in agriculture and her Gross National Product (GNP) *per capita* was only about 60 per cent of that enjoyed in the UK. Ireland was handicapped by a lack of mineral resources, low industrialisation, a small domestic market, a high birthrate and a relatively small ratio of employed persons to the total population. The first Irish government accepted the reality of Irish dependence by tying their new currency to sterling and adopting a policy of free trade.

There was little change in the Irish economic situation until 1932, when the passionately anti-British de Valera became Prime Minister and launched his country into an 'economic war' with the UK. Protective tariffs were imposed and retaliatory measures were quickly taken by the British Government. The immediate effects of this development on the Irish economy were unfortunate. The cattle industry 'was threatened with collapse' (Lyons, p. 612); exports declined drastically; the balance of payments developed a serious deficit; and the country did not free itself from dependence on the British market since at no time during the 1930s did the percentage of its exports going there fall below 90. It was with some relief that in 1938 the Irish reached an agreement with the British Government whereby their trading relations would revert to the position of early 1932.

On the other hand, the period of protection stimulated the growth of small industrial concerns and the number of people employed in industry rose by exactly 50 per cent during the period (see Lyons, p. 619). Furthermore, the Irish Government created a number of state enterprises which were to be the forerunners, not of a move towards nationalisation and socialism, but of a move towards state planning and assistance to industry.

The wartime period somewhat increased the self-sufficiency of the Irish economy, but there was no major change in economic policy until 1958. The impetus for the change that then occurred came from the failure of Ireland to share in the rapid increase in living standards that most Western European countries enjoyed during the 1950s. The relevant figures are given in Table 5.1.

This failure was reflected in a rapid increase in emigration. The exceptionally high nineteenth-century rate of emigration from Ireland had been greatly reduced in the early years of the

Table 5.1   *Personal Consumption per Capita in Various European Countries, 1950–8*

Country	1950	1958
Ireland	163	170
Italy	127	170
Germany (Federal Republic)	185	303
Netherlands	202	233
France	221	298
Belgium	250	276
United Kingdom	290	327

Source: Chubb, p. 329.

twentieth century as a consequence of land reforms and the purchase of farms and smallholdings following the Conservative Government's Land Act of 1903. But it remained the aim of Irish political leaders to reduce emigration still further and the rapid increase during the 1950s was viewed with alarm. It was partly because of this alarm that the Irish Government introduced a series of economic planning measures in 1958 which transformed the economy in the following fifteen years. The emigration figures are given in Table 5.2.

Table 5.2   *Net Emigration from the Irish Republic*

Period	Rate per year per 1000 inhabitants
1926–36	5·6
1936–46	6·3
1946–51	8·2
1951–6	13·4
1956–61	14·8
1961–6	5·7
1966–71	4·1

Source: Chubb, p. 326.

The economic planners and politicians who tackled Irish problems in the late fifties had to face the fact that a country with no mineral resources and a small population is intrinsically handicapped in its attempts to industrialise. The absence of mineral resources deprives it of cheap fuel or steel and makes it dependent on imported raw materials. The domestic market is too small to support industries based on advanced technology and mass production. The planners decided to meet this situation by attempting to attract overseas industrial firms to establish plants in Ireland making goods designed primarily for export. They calculated, correctly, that Ireland had several points of appeal for international firms, including: (1) the existence of a stable political system; (2) the absence of militant trade unions and the fact that neither of the two main parties is committed to nationalisation or other socialist objectives; (3) a plentiful supply of labour; (4) the use of English as the main language; and (5) the fact that Ireland is an attractive area of residence for business executives.

Measures adopted in 1958 included a five-year plan, the passage of the Encouragement of External Investment Act, and the creation of the Industrial Development Authority (IDA). The IDA has established overseas offices and offers expert assistance to industrial firms which are contemplating or might be persuaded to contemplate investment in Ireland. The incentives to which the IDA can point include the following:

(1)   Complete exemption from tax on profits generated by exports for fifteen years (though not beyond 1990).
(2)   Non-repayable grants towards the costs of new fixed assets, such as land, buildings and machinery, of up to 50 per cent in designated areas of the country (mainly in the west) and 35 per cent elsewhere except in Dublin (where no grants are payable).
(3)   Grants for the training of workers.
(4)   Grants for research and development.

In special cases the IDA can also offer credit facilities and the use of advance factories built out of public funds. It should be noted that all the above incentives are subject to negotiation between the IDA and the individual firm, apart from the exemption from profits tax on exports, which firms can claim as of right. In the Irish-speaking districts the Gaeltarra Eireann performs the same functions as the IDA and can offer more generous terms.

These policies were extremely successful. In the years 1960–73 Ireland enjoyed a growth in productivity (Gross Domestic Product per person employed) of 9·1 per cent, which was equal to that of the German Federal Republic and surpassed in the EEC only by France (9·9 per cent) and Italy (11·4 per cent). This compared with a growth in productivity in the UK of only 5·5 per cent. The growth of industrial output in these years was at the rate of approximately 6 per cent per annum and if 1960 is taken as a baseline the index of output of manufactured goods had risen to 222 by 1973. The importance of the new policies introduced in 1958 is further demonstrated by Table 5.3, which puts the progress made into historical perspective.

Table 5.3 *Economic Growth in the Irish Republic, 1926–73*

| | Annual Rates of Growth of GNP at Factor Cost | | | | | | |
	1926–31	1931–8	1938–50	1950–8	1958–68	1968–73	1926–73
Average annual percentage rate of growth	2·4	− 0·4	1·5	− 0·3	4·4	4·7	1·9

Source: O'Hagan, p. 117.

The above figures have been taken only to 1973 because the drastic rise in oil prices in that year affected Ireland as it affected other European countries. Moreover, as the Irish pound, though not legally tied to sterling since 1971, is in fact kept at parity with sterling by the international money market, the Irish economy has been adversely influenced by the rapid devaluation of sterling since 1974. Ireland's partial dependence on the sagging British market, which still takes slightly more than half her exports, has also made it difficult for her to adjust to the higher level of fuel prices as well as most Continental countries have done. Between 1973 and 1976 prices and unemployment rose as sharply as they did in Britain and there was no significant economic growth.

Nevertheless, the experience of the years 1958–73 is highly encouraging. The economic progress of those years was a real breakthrough. It showed that the adoption of shrewd economic policies could achieve a substantial measure of economic independence and success even for what a French commentator has called 'an island off an island', with a small home market and few natural resources. This achievement has proved that independence can bring not only the political benefits of self-government but also a faster rate of economic growth than that of the country which dominated Ireland for so long.

THE PROBLEMS OF NORTHERN IRELAND

The partition of Ireland created a province whose population was divided on religious and political lines just as clearly as the population of a united Ireland would have been divided on religious and political lines. The problems arising from this cleavage seem at the time of writing to be insoluble, and many would say that partition has been a failure.

It should not be thought that Ireland is unique in this respect.

The partition of India in 1947 caused over a million deaths in the massacres and transfers of population that followed, and the two states created have engaged in warfare since. The partitions of Korea and Vietnam were followed in each case by a major war. The elaborate arrangements for a partial segregation of the two ethnic communities in Cyprus have not proved lasting, and have been followed by a more drastic partition which has caused and is causing much suffering. Partition is best regarded as a desperate measure to deal with desperate problems, which are unlikely to be solved completely by the split. The main justification of partition in Ireland, as in India, must be that without it the consequences of communal conflict would have spread more widely and caused even more suffering.

The social divisions between Protestants and Catholics in Northern Ireland are extraordinarily deep. The churches have an importance in Irish life that is quite astonishing to a contemporary Englishman. Surveys of church attendance in England, conducted in the late 1940s, showed that about 12 per cent of the adult population attended church on a normal Sunday. The figure has fallen since that date and the proportion of young people attending church is certainly much lower than that. But a survey of university students in Belfast in 1959 showed that 94 per cent of Catholics and between 50 and 55 per cent of Protestants claimed to have attended church the *previous* Sunday (Barritt and Carter, p. 21). A more recent survey of the population showed that 62 per cent of Catholics and 46 per cent of Protestants claimed to attend church at least once a week (Rose (*b*), p. 12). Moreover, many social and recreational activities that are in most societies completely independent of the churches are in Northern Ireland organised by the churches.

All schools have a religious affiliation and there is complete segregation between Protestants and Catholics in the schools they attend. The schools organise different sports, so Catholics and Protestants never meet on the sports field. They also differ in their treatment of history: the Protestant schools are mainly concerned with British history, which (given the nature of the textbooks) is essentially English history; the Catholic schools place much more emphasis on Irish history, which tends to be largely a history of Irish struggles against British oppression. There is considerable segregation in areas of residence and in clubs and pubs visited. There is little inter-marriage, which is discouraged by Protestants and denounced by Catholics. There is a great deal of segregation in employment. The animosity which characterises inter-communal relations is sharpened by the long historical memories from which all Irishmen seem to suffer. These extend right back to the seventeenth century, when the conflict was more one between natives and settlers than between two branches of the Christian religion.

In many respects the conflict still resembles an ethnic or tribal conflict. Like tribes, each community has its own myths and heroes, its own songs and its own symbols – the orange and green sashes, the Union Jack and the Irish tricolour. Each community also has its own ritual marches, which by celebrating past victories are designed to rub salt in the wounds of the other side. The delicate art of political provocation has its most devoted exponents in Belfast. Thus, the display and parade of the Irish tricolour was frequently used to anger Protestants, who saw it as an open display of disloyalty. In 1954 it was made illegal to fly the flag, if done in circumstances likely to cause a breach of the peace. Once this Act was passed Protestant gangs often made sure that it caused a breach of the peace, even if flown in solidly Catholic areas. The question of Sunday games has caused constant irritation, as Catholics regard Sunday afternoon as an occasion for recreation and Protestants have used their control of the City Council to prohibit the use of municipal parks or playing-fields on the Sabbath. When the Gaelic Athletic Association acquired its own football ground in Belfast to get over this ban, it was called the Roger Casement Park to serve as a constant reminder to Protestants of the Ulsterman who was executed for treason by the British in 1916. In 1940–1, when Hitler had conquered Europe and Britain stood alone, the slogan 'England's extremity – Ireland's opportunity' was painted on Belfast walls.

It was inevitable that the social cleavage would be reflected in the political system. A completely unintegrated society cannot be expected to produce integrated political parties. The best that could be hoped in such a situation (assuming political integration to be desirable) is that a system of accommodation would develop whereby representatives of both communities would be given some say (though not necessarily an equal say) in the government of the province. In Canada, Switzerland, Holland and several other countries a deliberate attempt has been made to ensure that no community or group is completely excluded from political power. In Canada, for instance, there is a convention that, no matter which party holds office, the federal cabinet should if possible contain more than one French-speaking Catholic, at least one English-speaking Catholic, and representatives from each region of the country.

In Northern Ireland no such conventions developed. The

overwhelming majority of Protestant voters supported the Ulster Unionist Party at each election, and as 65 per cent of the voters are Protestant that party had a comfortable majority throughout the life of the Stormont Parliament. Any possibility that the Unionists might share power or influence with their opponents, even in a very minor way, was removed by the attitude taken by Catholic politicians. In the first elections to the Stormont Parliament the Unionists won 40 seats and their opponents won 12 (equally divided between Sinn Fein and a new Nationalist Party). These twelve all refused to take their seats on the ground that they refused to acknowledge the legitimacy of partition and therefore of the new Parliament. Though some Catholic MPs took their seats in later years, the main policy objective of the Catholic parties has always been the abolition of the Stormont Parliament and the incorporation of Northern Ireland into the Republic. Unionist politicians naturally regarded this as a form of disloyalty which disqualified Catholic politicians from any form of participation in the governmental system.

The elaborate system of devolution from Westminster to Stormont therefore meant devolution to a province dominated by a single party. Dominance by one party over long periods is apt to lead to exploitation of power, even when the tensions between the parties are much less acute than in Northern Ireland. Labour Party dominance over several decades has led to corruption in local government in the north-east of England and in parts of South Wales. In Northern Ireland the Unionists have been accused of: (1) rigging the electoral system; (2) gerrymandering in local government; (3) packing the judiciary and the police with Protestants; and (4) discrimination in the administration of social services. There is some truth in these allegations, though not so much as opposition propaganda suggests.

(1) This allegation is based on the fact that in 1929 the Unionists abolished the use of proportional representation in elections to Stormont and replaced it by an electoral system similar to that used in Britain. Their main reason for making this change was to discourage the growth of minor parties which might split the Protestant vote, but the move did not make any significant difference to the representation of the Catholic community, as eleven Nationalist or Republican candidates were returned at the two general elections following the change compared with the twelve who had been returned in the two elections before the change.

(2) In local government elections Stormont failed to adopt the reform made elsewhere in the United Kingdom in 1948, whereby

the ratepayer franchise was replaced by universal suffrage. The reason was that the ratepayer franchise gave an electoral advantage to the Unionists because a greater proportion of Protestants than of Catholics paid rates. In several areas the ward boundaries were also drawn in such a way as to help the Unionists, the most notable example being Londonderry, where careful gerrymandering ensured a permanent Unionist majority on the City Council in spite of the fact that 60 per cent of the citizens were Catholic.

(3) In 1969 nine-tenths of the lawyers holding posts in the judiciary were Protestants, and it has been suggested that the governments responsible for these appointments have shown 'favouritism to Protestants' (see Harbinson, p. 119). The figures do not prove this, as it is possible that Catholic lawyers have preferred to maintain their independence of a governmental system that some of them regard as illegitimate. But this would be no consolation to Catholics appearing in court who may feel that the judicial system is weighted against them.

The Catholic community has also been worried about the composition of the Royal Ulster Constabulary (RUC), which has never been less than 88 per cent Protestant. In fact, one of the first decisions of the Stormont Government was to reserve one-third of the places in the RUC for Catholics, but Nationalist politicians discouraged their followers from joining and the quota had to be abandoned. The Unionists cannot therefore be criticised for the composition of the RUC, though the fact that it has always been overwhelmingly Protestant has led to constant complaints of discriminatory behaviour, some of which have been valid.

(4) There has been clear discrimination by local authorities in the allocation of municipal housing. Catholic authorities discriminate just as much as Protestant authorities, but as most authorities have been controlled by Protestant politicians, and as Catholics have proportionately greater need of municipal housing, the overall consequence has been to the disadvantage of the Catholic community. There is no discrimination in most social services, as these are governed by United Kingdom legislation which has been adopted without revision by Stormont. However, this does not prevent controversy, particularly over the vexed question of family size. A Nationalist politician told me that the regulations regarding Supplementary Benefits are unfair to Catholics, since claimants with large families suffer grave hardship because of the 'wages stop', whereby the highest rate of benefit has to remain less than the lowest wage in the area. A Unionist politician, on the other hand, told me that the generous

rate of benefit for people with large families discourages many Catholics from seeking work. The truth of the matter is that in such cases the wages stop is adjusted upwards to take account of the Family Income Supplement that lower-paid workers with large families can claim, but the system is sufficiently mysterious to allow both resentments to continue unchecked.

The political situation in Northern Ireland has been more or less tense since devolution came into effect in 1921 and the Catholic minority in the province have always been more or less discontented. They have felt themselves to be second-class citizens, permanently excluded from political power, and held in some contempt by the majority. In a survey of political attitudes conducted in 1968, 56 per cent of Catholics interviewed were in favour of the abolition of 'the border', compared with 32 per cent against this and 12 per cent who did not know (Rose (a), p. 213). Since incorporation into the Republic would mean a reduction in the overall standard of living (following the loss of British subsidies) by about a fifth, it is possible to argue that a majority of Catholic citizens at that time would have been willing to accept a severe reduction in living standards for the sake of living in a Catholic rather than a Protestant state. Such an argument would be rash, however, as expressing dislike of the border when interviewed is itself costless. Catholics who strongly dislike the regime in the North can move to the Republic, since they enjoy dual citizenship, but only a few do so. A question about the constitution of Northern Ireland produced a threefold division among Catholics, with about a third expressing approval, a third expressing disapproval, and the remaining third uncertain (Rose (a), p. 189); and this is probably a better guide to the distribution of attitudes than the answers to the question about the border. In a survey in 1974 only 23 per cent of Catholics gave unity with the Republic as their first choice for the future of Northern Ireland (NOP survey), and it is probably best to abandon the search for exact figures and to say that between a fifth and a third of the Catholic community apparently want unification.

Despite this partial alienation of the minority, the position in Northern Ireland in the mid-sixties gave more cause for hope than at any previous time. The Prime Minister, Terence O'Neill, was the most liberal leader the Ulster Unionists have ever had, and his main object from 1963 to 1968 was to improve relations with the Republic and (in his words) to 'build bridges' to the Catholic minority in the North. On the other side, the IRA was weaker than it had ever been since 1922 and there were several

Catholic leaders who were willing to attend Stormont and play a constructive role there. Why, therefore, did the political situation suddenly deteriorate in 1968–9, leading to the virtual disintegration of Northern Ireland as a political society?

The answer to the question falls into two parts. First, O'Neill's liberalism caused a minor backlash among the Protestant community. He was able to carry many middle-class Unionists with him, but working-class and rural Protestants were deeply suspicious of his activities. As he acknowledged: 'It is frightfully hard to explain to Protestants that if you give Roman Catholics a good job and a good house, they will live like Protestants' (quoted in Paor, p. 125). A militant Protestant leader appeared in the person of the Rev. Ian Paisley, whose attitude to O'Neill's 'bridge-building' activities was brutally simple: 'A traitor and a bridge are very much alike, for they both go over to the other side' (quoted in Rose (a), p. 101). There were demonstrations and clear signs of a hardening of attitudes.

The second development was more novel and more critical. In 1967 the Civil Rights Association (CRA) was formed by university students in Belfast, and planned a crusade in Northern Ireland based on the example of the Civil Rights movement in the United States. Its original membership consisted not only of Irish nationalists but also of radical socialists and idealistic reformers, similar to the groups who were active in British student politics at the same time. But its concern was essentially for the rights of the Catholic minority; it was naturally perceived by others as a nationalist group; and it was quickly infiltrated by IRA members. In October 1968 it was joined by a more overtly revolutionary organisation called People's Democracy (PD). The tactic adopted by the CRA and PD leaders was to provoke violence by their opponents and the police in the expectation that they would thereby win sympathy and support not only from the Catholic community but also from British and international opinion. In the explosive political atmosphere of Northern Ireland this tactic worked brilliantly.

Political marches have such a long history in Northern Ireland that they have acquired the character of a political institution, with their own rules and conventions. The basic rule is that they take place mainly in 'home territory' but go to the border, and perhaps just over the border, of 'enemy territory' to annoy and provoke the other community. But a Catholic march which was planned to go right through a Protestant area, or vice versa, would normally be rerouted by the police and this would be accepted. The tactic of the CRA was to claim they were a nonsectarian organisation and therefore not bound by the convention.

In 1968 the CRA gave notice of a march in Londonderry on 5 October which was not only to be in a Protestant part of the city but was also to follow a traditional route of Protestant marches, ending by the War Memorial. Unionists protested, the Minister of Home Affairs (William Craig) banned the march, and the Nationalist leader at Stormont (Eddie McAteer) asked the CRA to call off the march. But the CRA went ahead in defiance of the ban and took the march deliberately into a cordon of police who had orders to stop it. There ensued a running fight in narrow streets between police swinging batons and demonstrators using banners, bricks and stones as weapons. Many people were injured, and films of the fighting were shown all over the British Isles on television as apparent evidence of police brutality.

After several further skirmishes in the autumn, PD decided to stage a march of eighty miles from Belfast to Londonderry in January 1969, passing through territory that was nearly all Protestant. Nationalist leaders again asked the organisers to call the march off and were again ignored. This march was not banned, as the authorities knew that the October riot had been a propaganda victory for the CRA. But eight miles outside Londonderry the marchers were attacked by a mob of militant Protestants armed with stones and cudgels. The police had warned the marchers of the ambush but remained neutral while the fighting ensued, an attitude that was not strictly correct but was understandable as many of the marshals on the march were IRA men known to the police from previous encounters. They remained neutral also as the battered marchers entered Londonderry, followed by their assailants, and both sides were reinforced by local residents in a free-for-all which lasted for hours. But after midnight many of the police joined in on the Protestant side and were subsequently censured for this by the report of an official inquiry (Cameron Report, para. 177). Again, the final result of the affair was a propaganda victory for the demonstrators and the erosion of the reputation and authority of the RUC.

The next major step in the lurch to chaos and disintegration occurred in August 1969. By this time the liberal Captain O'Neill had been forced to resign as Prime Minister and had been replaced by Major Chichester-Clark, a more traditional Unionist who was not so keen on building bridges to the Catholic community. On the 281st anniversary of the Apprentice Boys' victory in Londonderry (12 August) the Protestant organisations staged a bigger parade than usual in that city, but were met with unprecedented militancy and organisation on the part of the Catholics. A full-scale riot ensued in which Catholics armed with stones and petrol bombs made out of milk bottles fought police armed with batons and CS gas. Barricades were erected and burnt down, scores of people were injured, the police could not control the situation, and eventually the Government of Northern Ireland asked the British Government to send troops to restore order. The report that the local dairy lost 43,000 milk bottles indicates the scale of the violence (Rose (a), p. 106).

Still nobody had died, but this record was not to last long. The spectacle of Catholic demonstrators throwing petrol bombs at the police, shown in close-up on television screens throughout the country, was too much for the militant Protestants of Belfast – particularly since the Catholics appeared to be getting the better of the battle. When Catholics in Belfast set up barricades (including hijacked buses) on 14 August, the RUC and the Special Constabulary opened fire and were followed into the Catholic areas by Protestant mobs armed with petrol bombs. In the ensuing riots 7 people were killed (5 Catholics and 2 Protestants), over 100 suffered gunshot wounds, and well over 200 houses (nearly all Catholic) were destroyed by fire. Peace was restored only when British troops arrived in force to separate the contestants and protect the Catholic areas.

This was the beginning of the end of the political system through which Northern Ireland had been governed since devolution was introduced in 1920. By 1970 there were four private armies in operation: the Official IRA, the more extreme Provisional IRA, the Protestant Ulster Defence Association (UDA), and the more extreme Ulster Volunteer Force (UVF). Between 1969 and the end of 1976, 1702 people were killed by political violence in Northern Ireland together with 62 in England and 40 in the Republic, while thousands were seriously injured. In proportion to population, these deaths in Northern Ireland are equivalent to about 60,000 deaths in Britain or 235,000 in the United States. (For comparison, the American death-roll in Vietnam was 43,000.)

It is not intended to summarise developments since 1969, which have been reported extensively and have not yet reached a point of stability. But it is relevant to indicate some of the lessons that can be learnt from these developments.

The first lesson is to underline an obvious truth: that in a state or province where the legitimacy of the regime is not accepted by a sizeable minority of the population, there is an inherent tendency for political conflict to occur in the streets rather than in the legislative assembly. The problems of government in this kind of situation have been admirably analysed in Richard Rose's *Governing without Consensus.*

The second lesson is the vulnerability of a democratic regime when threatened by private armies, and the durability of the latter once they are established. Neither Northern Ireland nor the Republic has been able to get rid of the IRA and the Protestant para-military forces, though never yet involved in a substantial military action, have existed since 1912 as a potential threat. Many of the 40,000 guns that were imported by the Ulster Volunteers in 1912 are thought still to be usable, having been kept under floorboards and greased with loving care ever since, and more modern weapons have been acquired recently. They haunt the minds of the Catholic community, as indicated by the chorus of a well-known Republican song:

> We'll haul down the barricades
> And call in our sons
> When a hundred thousand Loyalists
> Hand in their guns.

This chorus neatly illustrates the effects of violence (or threats of violence) by members of one community on the attitudes of the other community. The exact number of usable guns is not important, so long as there are enough to sustain the fears of the potential victims. Moreover, there were over 200 actual victims, individual Catholics assassinated by Protestant extremists, in the period 1974–6 – a slightly higher total than the number of Protestants personally assassinated by Catholics in the same period (deaths as a result of bombs, booby traps and other terrorist tactics being excluded from these figures).

Another effect of private armies is the spread of protection rackets, armed robberies, and disciplinary violence within each community. All these are now rife in Belfast, and in 1975 politicians on both sides told me spontaneously of their concern about the increasing criminality of their own para-military forces and the degrading effect this has on day-to-day life in the working-class areas.

A third lesson is the extent to which the mass media, and especially television, can be exploited by troublemakers. The sight of police wielding batons or throwing gas cannisters at a crowd which includes women and children has an emotional impact which can undo years of careful police work and good public relations. The BBC has horrified many people in Northern Ireland by its policy of neutrality in the conflict, so that IRA leaders are interviewed on the same basis as government ministers, panic is spread by pictures of burning houses, and alarm is created by feature programmes on the secret training camps of Protestant para-military forces. This policy was deliberately adopted by the BBC after internal discussions in 1969, according to its news and current affairs editor. To maintain their reputation for impartial journalism, they decided they had to avoid any form of self-censorship and to cover whatever was newsworthy.

If at times this policy has helped the IRA, at other times it has helped the Protestant extremists. During the Ulster Workers' Strike of May 1974, BBC Radio was the main source of local news. In that crisis, it is said that public opinion was greatly influenced by the almost hourly predictions made on the radio by an electricity board official that there was to be an immediate and complete cut-off of power throughout the province. This was quite untrue, 'but it provided the most potent symbol of the strike: the inevitability of catastrophe if the Executive remained in office. It was a message which the BBC, in its news broadcasts, its magazine programmes, its interviews and its on-the-spot reports, repeated again and again' (Fisk, p. 140). Given the policies of the BBC, this kind of reporting can only be stopped by government censorship, which is repugnant in a democracy not actually at war, but there can be no doubt of the help it gives the disruptive or revolutionary groups who know how to exploit its possibilities.

A fourth lesson is the exceptionally difficult task faced by security forces operating in a democratic society against revolutionaries who enjoy the sympathy of a section of the people. To put this in perspective, it is worth listing the objectives of the Republican organisations in Northern Ireland.

(1) To erode the authority of the police. (Achieved, 1968–9.)
(2) To provoke Protestant extremists into a backlash that would cause communal violence and a breakdown of law and order. (Achieved, August 1969.)
(3) To erode the authority of the Stormont Government and Parliament. (Achieved, 1969–72.)
(4) To provoke the British Army into repressive tactics which would solidify Catholic resistance, would lead to international protests and might cause a revulsion of feeling in Britain.

(5) To make the British public and government so disgusted with Irish politics that they hand over Northern Ireland to Dublin.

Having some understanding of these objectives, the Army has kept a low profile and its 15,000 troops have acted with a high degree of discipline under very strict rules. They may not open fire unless life is directly threatened; they may fire only at a specific and identified target, not blindly into a crowd; they have to account in writing for each bullet fired; and if they exceed their instructions they may be liable to criminal prosecution as well as to military discipline. The consequence is that the loss of life has been kept to a minimum and (at some cost to its effectiveness) the Army has won the propaganda battle in Britain and overseas.

In the Catholic areas, however, the Army could not hope for support, once the immediate threat from Protestant mobs was controlled. Traditional hostility to the sight of British troops rose to a crescendo when internment was introduced in August 1971, because of the difficulty of getting convictions in the courts. This move was a propaganda gift to the IRA, which it exploited in predictable ways. It is worth quoting several lines from a song that was sung in Catholic clubs and pubs after internment, to a rousing tune, because it illustrates not only the particular issue but also (once again) the Irish sense of history and the sense or resentment at being treated as inferiors.

> Through the little streets of Belfast
> In the dark of early morn
> British soldiers came marauding
> Wrecking little homes with scorn.
> Heedless of the crying children
> Dragging fathers from their beds
> Beating sons while helpless mothers
> Watched the blood pour from their heads.
>
> Armoured cars and tanks and guns
> Came to take away our sons
> But every man will stand behind
> The men behind the wire.
>
> Not for them a judge and jury
> Nor indeed a crime at all
> Being Irish means they're guilty
> So to we're guilty one and all.
> Round the world the truth will echo

> Cromwell's men are here again
> England's name again is sullied
> In the eyes of honest men.
>
> Armoured cars and tanks and guns
> Came to take away our sons
> But every man will stand behind
> The men behind the wire.

Internment brought a flood of recruits to the IRA and for at least a year, and perhaps two, the maintenance of security was much more difficult. In 1973, and even more in 1974, the Army managed to get on top of the situation, with better intelligence which enabled them to distinguish the hard-core IRA gunmen from the unskilled recruits who had got caught up in the movement. But the IRA has another tactic which is used when the Army looks like winning, namely to call a truce and demand the release of detainees. Since no democratic politician wants to keep people interned indefinitely, the authorities have accepted these demands and the IRA has had a breathing space in which to regroup for the next offensive. In this kind of political situation it is impossible for the Army to achieve what is sometimes called 'a military solution', that is, to destroy the IRA.

The logic of this argument points to a political compromise as the only hope for the achievement of stability. But a fifth lesson, learnt many times in other countries also, is that moderate politicians are the first casualties of violence. British governments have been trying since 1973 to persuade the Ulster Unionists to engage in some form of 'power-sharing' with their political opponents, but one consequence of the years of violence is that leadership within the Unionist camp has passed progressively from more liberal to less liberal men. The bridge-building Terence O'Neill was replaced by the less liberal James Chichester-Clark, who was in turn replaced by Brian Faulkner. When William Whitelaw and Edward Heath persuaded Faulkner to lead a power-sharing executive he was first expelled by his party and then forced to resign by a general strike of Protestant workers. This left William Craig, previously regarded as a 'hard-liner', as the most experienced leader on the Unionist side, and when he was persuaded by the logic of the situation to endorse some ingenious plans for a new form of power-sharing he was in turn expelled by his party. By November 1975 Ian Paisley, the anti-Papist crusader, was the effective leader of the Unionists.

This ratchet-like set of developments naturally represented a series of setbacks to British policy-makers, whose attitudes and behaviour will be examined in Chapter 8. But the process which led to these successive shifts of power is perfectly intelligible. The consequence is that it is now very difficult to foresee Northern Ireland moving to a political situation that is as peaceful and democratic as that which existed in 1967, unsatisfactory as that was to the minority. The six counties, unlike the Republic, still seem to deserve Louis MacNeice's sad comment:

> I come from an island, Ireland, a nation
> Built upon violence and morose vendettas.
> My diehard countrymen like drayhorses
> Drag their ruin behind them.
> Shooting straight in the cause of crooked thinking
> . . .
> From all which I am an exile.

6
Scottish Nationalism

There is a distinction between national self-consciousness and nationalism which is particularly important in the case of Scotland. Virtually all Scotsmen are conscious of being Scottish, but only a minority of them (so far) are Scottish nationalists. The firm sense of national identity which Scotsmen enjoy derives partly from the long history of Scotland's existence as an independent nation-state before the union with England and partly from the fact that many Scottish institutions have remained intact and distinctive since the union.

The Scottish Parliament was virtually the only Scottish institution to be abolished by the 1707 Act of Union (or Treaty of Union as it is sometimes called north of the border). The Scottish legal system was preserved, a matter of importance not only because of the differences in law between the two countries but also because it reserved the practice of Scottish law for Scotsmen and maintained Edinburgh as a centre of the legal profession, comparable with London in this respect but unlike Cardiff. The Presbyterian Church of Scotland remained the established church and the English made no attempt, as they did in Ireland and Wales, to impose the Church of England. The influence of the Church of Scotland has been extensive and its General Assembly has served as a forum for the expression of Scottish opinion not only on theological matters but also on a variety of social and political issues.

The Scottish educational system was also preserved and until as recently as the 1940s it was widely thought to be superior to the English system. The schools in Scotland have not been secularised, as they have in England; they have not gone in for such early specialisation; and their syllabuses and examinations are rather different. Until the 1930s Scotland had four universities to England's two, and although England now has many more universities the proportion of Scottish school-leavers who go on to university is still much higher than the equivalent proportion in England.

These institutions have helped to preserve the distinctions between Scottish and English society and to maintain a clear sense of national self-conciousness in Scotland. This sense is also sustained by the focus on Scottish affairs shown in Scottish newspapers and the abundance of national symbols. The Scots are quite exceptionally well endowed in this respect, having not only a national flag but also national clothing, food, drink, dances, music, games and literature. They are certainly better endowed than the English, who are conspicuously short of symbols which are English without being British.

In view of all these factors, it is easy to understand why the Scots have a clear (and constitutionally correct) sense of national identity. They see themselves as Scottish first and British second, the one referring to their membership of a national society and the other to their citizenship in a multi-national state. Research by social psychologists has shown that Scottish children progress from an early identification of Scotland as 'their country' to a later acknowledgement that they are British, while English children tend to use the words 'English' and 'British' interchangeably throughout their teens – and indeed continue to do so throughout their lives (see Jahoda; Dennis). For different reasons, the Welsh and (as we have seen) the Northern Irish senses of national identity are also less clear than the Scottish sense.

Scottish nationalism, while being nationalism of an aspiring rather than a possessive type, therefore had firm foundations on which to build. Scottish nationalists have had no need to awaken a sense of national pride, for that has existed for centuries. However, it was not until as recently as the 1960s that a nationalist movement, in the strict sense of a movement demanding national independence for Scotland, became an effective political force, and not until the 1970s that it won widespread support.

There had indeed been numerous demands in earlier years for the creation of a Scottish Assembly to control domestic affairs. Between 1886 and 1928 fourteen separate bills to establish a Scottish Assembly or Parliament were introduced in the House of Commons, though none of them was passed. These earlier movements have been admirably chronicled in H. J. Hanham's *Scottish Nationalism* and it is unnecessary to repeat the story here. It will be more helpful to concentrate our attention on the question of why the intermittent rumblings of Scottish discontent with the British system of government should have been transformed in the last few years into an active demand for Scottish independence by a nationalist party which was supported by just over 30 per cent of Scottish voters at the general election of October 1974.

The headings under which an answer may be sought are fairly

obvious, deriving as they do from experience of nationalist movements in various parts of the world. They may be summarised as follows:

(1) resentment of cultural domination and threats to a traditional way of life;
(2) resentment of political discrimination which denies liberties or proper representation to the national minority;
(3) resentment of economic domination and the belief that the national minority is denied a fair share of the benefits of industrial growth;
(4) the expectation of economic or diplomatic advantages to be gained from independence.

These headings will serve for the discussion of the rise of nationalism in both Scotland and Wales.

Cultural Domination
Under the first of these headings, which is important in the case of Wales, we can only enter a 'nil return' for Scotland. The success of the Lowland Scots in virtually eliminating the Gaelic language on the Scottish mainland removed an issue which might in other circumstances have become a nationalist issue. Although the Scottish National Party (SNP) wishes to preserve Gaelic in those limited areas where it is spoken, it has no intention of trying to revive the language for widespread use on the mainland. And there are certainly no linguistic issues between Scotland and England.

Most observers would say that there are some quite significant cultural differences between Scottish and English society which have nothing to do with language, but these are not easy to define. Some interesting evidence of differences in behaviour has emerged from the National Child Development Study, a research project which is tracing the development of a large national sample of children born in the same week of March 1958. It was found that when these children were seven years old the Scottish children were on average half an inch shorter than the English children and two pounds lighter, with children in the south of England tending to be slightly taller and heavier than those in the north (see Pringle). However, the Scottish children were markedly more stable than the English ones, displaying less tendency to bite their nails, suffer from headaches or sleeplessness, have nightmares, dislike their school, behave in a disobedient or destructive way, fight with other children or have temper tantrums. In every one of these symptoms there was a clear geographical progression from north to south, with children in the northern regions of England being less stable and happy than Scottish children but better adjusted than those further south. Welsh children came between northern English children and southern English children in these respects, exactly as geography would indicate.

These regional differences were not caused by socio-economic factors and indeed ran counter to them, for within each area the children of manual workers tended to be less well adjusted than other children and Scotland and northern England have a higher proportion of manual workers in the population (and in the sample) than more southerly regions. The conclusion reached by the research team was that the main reason for the differences was parental behaviour, with parents in Scotland and the north spending more time with their children and taking more interest in their schooling and progress. This research therefore supplies some justification for the feelings of moral superiority that some Scots people and some northerners display towards 'the soft and degenerate south'.

At the same time, the statistics also suggest that the difference is not one between national societies so much as one between geographical areas. The data can be interpreted as demonstrating national differences if the line is drawn at the border and the figures for the English regions are aggregated, but give a different impression if the English figures are not aggregated.

If the data are interpreted in national terms, they support the generalisation that Scottish parents tend to be less permissive and more old-fashioned than English parents. This goes along with the fact that there tends to be stricter discipline in Scottish schools, where much more use is made of corporal punishment. It also coheres with the greater importance of religion in Scottish life and with the prevalence of certain puritanical tendencies – though the latter do not go unchallenged.

However, differences of this kind do not create political grievances as they are reflected in legal and institutional differences under the present system of government. For instance, the rules about punishments in schools are different, the marriage and divorce laws are different, homosexual relations between consenting adults are still illegal in Scotland, the licensing laws are more restrictive, and it is actually against the law for alcohol to be consumed on motor coaches.

Political Discrimination

On the face of things, there is little evidence for the view that the Scots are unfairly treated under the British political system. Scotland has been over-represented in the House of Commons throughout the twentieth century and this practice was institutionalised in 1944, when separate boundary commissions were established for England, Wales, Scotland and Northern Ireland. If Scotland had the same ratio of seats to electors as England it would now have only 57 seats, whereas in fact it has 71. The argument that this is justified by the sparse population of Scottish rural areas can account for only a small proportion of this difference – perhaps for four or five of the fourteen extra seats. Scottish urban areas also benefit: if Glasgow had the same ratio of seats to electors as Birmingham there would be ten Glasgow constituencies whereas in fact there are thirteen. In the twentieth century Scotland has always had at least one representative (and has usually had more) in the British Cabinet, and it has also provided five of the seventeen prime ministers who have held office since 1900.

Within Parliament, there is the Scottish Grand Committee (established 1894) which contains all Scottish MPs and debates the majority of Scottish Bills at second reading, together with two Scottish Standing Committees (established 1957 and 1962) which conduct a detailed examination of the majority of Scottish Bills at the committee stage. However, these committees put a good deal of pressure on the time of Scottish MPs, and the Scottish Bills sometimes have to wait longer than United Kingdom Bills to find a place in the parliamentary timetable. There is also a problem when the majority of Scottish Members are opposed to the government of the day, which is not entirely overcome by the practice of adding English MPs to the Scottish Committees so as to ensure a government majority. For all these reasons, it has been said that 'in recent years . . . the machinery of Parliament has been inadequate to cope with the demands of Scottish legislation' (Kellas, p. 96).

There are also problems about the supervision of government activities in Scotland by Scottish MPs. Since the office of Secretary of State for Scotland was created in 1885, an increasing number of administrative activities have been handed over from British government departments to the Scottish Office, which has its main headquarters in Edinburgh. Administrative devolution of this kind has been greatly extended since 1945, so that the Scottish Secretary now has to answer to Parliament for a whole range of functions which include education, health, local government, law and order, road transport, agriculture and fisheries. But since ministers take turns on a rota to answer parliamentary questions, and the Scottish Secretary does so only once every three weeks, it is said to be more difficult for Scottish MPs to get attention to questions about administrative matters than it is for English MPs to do so (see Kellas, p. 96). In this way British attempts to meet the special needs of Scotland by administrative reforms have created fresh arguments for the establishment of a Scottish Parliament.

Economic Domination and the Distribution of Benefits
Under this heading it is helpful to distinguish between three phenomena, as follows:

(1) the possible distortion of the economy of a national community by external control of capital investment;
(2) the problems of economic inequality arising from uneven development;
(3) the impact of economic planning by the central government.

(1) Substantial capital investment from outside a national community is always apt to arouse fears of external control of economic development. But such investment conveys benefits as well as dangers and is rarely unwelcome when it is made. It is desirable either because it promotes developments which could not otherwise take place or because it compensates for deficits in the balance of trade. It becomes a genuine source of grievance only if it is used to distort the balance of the national economy in a way that harms the long-term interests of the local inhabitants.

In the case of Scotland it has been alleged not only by some Scottish writers but also by at least one American scholar that English control of capital development has distorted the Scottish economy by making it excessively specialised in its products and excessively dependent on overseas markets (see Hechter, *passim*). I do not find this argument very persuasive. First, Scotland was able to raise at least half the capital needed for the foundation of its major industries from Scottish sources, as well as to export considerable amounts of capital overseas, so it was not heavily dependent on English creditors. Secondly, although some Scottish industries (for example woollen textiles) suffered when the Union of 1707 ended their protection from English competition, their loss was balanced by the opening of the English market to other Scottish products, and in the nineteenth century industries in both countries benefited from the larger overall market.

Thirdly, it seems somewhat perverse to interpret the triumphant success of Scottish shipyards in the late nineteenth century as an English plot to make Scotland particularly vulnerable to Japanese competition in the mid-twentieth century. And finally, it is simply not the case that the modern Scottish economy suffers seriously from over-specialisation. It suffers from the decline of key industries but, as noted in Chapter 3, the distribution of employment between industries in Scotland is less specialised than in any other region of the United Kingdom.

However, it is clearly impossible to refute the proposition that capital investment from external sources carries with it the danger of external control over some aspects of the economy, and fears of this kind have naturally been reawakened by the massive investments in North Sea oil. These fears have been enhanced both by the suspicion that the London government will pay insufficient attention to the impact of the industry on Scottish communities and by reports that the Norwegian Government has taken more effective steps than the British Government to protect its people and their environment from the less desirable consequences of this impact.

(2) The problem of uneven development is unavoidable. In a common market, with free movement of labour and capital, there are bound to be differential rates of economic growth between regions. This was markedly the case during the nineteenth century, and in the *laissez-faire* system of that period the inevitable result was migration. However, it happened that the industrial developments of that century produced inequalities within each of Scotland, England and Wales that were more marked than the overall inequalities between these countries. Since 1918 the second industrial revolution has had a different geographical impact. The new industries are predominantly located in the midlands and south of England, while the staple industries of central Scotland and south Wales have declined. Although many of the industrial areas of northern England have suffered in the same way as Scotland and Wales, it is only natural that many Scots and Welsh people should think in national rather than regional terms and draw the conclusion that their countries have become economically disadvantaged in comparison with England.

Now, in a period of extensive government welfare services the poorer areas of a common market have much more to gain from a centralised system of government than they have from a system of devolved or federal government. Centralised administration involves an automatic process of fiscal equalisation, whereby the wealthiest areas contribute more in taxation and the poorer areas gain more from social benefits. Scotland and Wales therefore stand to benefit from the fairly centralised system of administration and taxation that exists in the United Kingdom, and there is evidence to show that they have benefited. Total government expenditure per head on local services was 31 per cent higher in Scotland than in England in 1967–70 and 27 per cent higher in 1975–6, although the English paid more per head in taxation (see Kilbrandon Report; *Hansard*, 29 November 1976).

Although Scottish nationalists sometimes complain about the distribution of government expenditure, this evidence does not suggest that they have a legitimate grievance on this score. Equally important, the opinion survey conducted for the Commission on the Constitution suggested that the Scottish people (and the Welsh) are somewhat more satisfied than the English with the quality of their public services.

Table 6.1   *Proportion of Citizens Describing
Their Public Services as 'Very Good'*

Service	England	Scotland	Wales
	%	%	%
Hospitals	50	62	48
Primary schools	26	36	32
Police	48	49	48
Electricity service	34	41	49
Postal service	34	37	41
Main roads	14	14	9
Weighted base	4,183	465	244
Unweighted number of respondents	3,274	892	726

Source: Commission on the Constitution, Research Paper 7, p. 53.

The figures in Table 6.1 are of course based on interviews with a random sample of the Scottish electorate and it is statistically possible that they conceal sharp differences of opinion, with SNP supporters having been strongly critical of the geographical distribution of government expenditure and the consequent level of government services in Scotland. Certainly SNP spokesmen have sometimes claimed that Scotland loses from the fiscal system, and during the 1960s it was not uncommon for SNP leaders to argue that a sizeable proportion of the revenues from Scottish taxpayers were spent outside Scotland. The third (1968) edition of *SNP and You: Aims and Policy of the Scottish National Party* claimed that in the sixteen years since 1952 £1,250 million of revenue from direct taxes in Scotland had been diverted in this way.

However, it is doubtful whether this line of argument has played any substantial part in the remarkable growth of the SNP since the 1960s. The claim was not greatly emphasised in the party's propaganda and no serious attempt was made to indicate its statistical basis, except by the suggestion that the Scottish contribution to UK defence contributions brought little benefit to the Scottish people. Some of the leading figures of the party during the 1960s supported the Campaign for Nuclear Disarmament and disapproved of the British contribution to NATO. But there is no evidence that the SNP has attracted its new voters from the left-wing fringes of the political spectrum: on the contrary, electoral statistics show that between 1966 and October 1974 it gained almost equally from the Conservative and Labour Parties (see Jaensch). During the 1970s the SNP has declared that its policy for an independent Scotland would include membership of NATO and in the detailed manifestoes the party issued for the two general elections of 1974 there was no repetition of the earlier claims that Scottish taxpayers were subsidising the English. Moreover, the claim was deleted from the fourth edition of *SNP and You*, published in 1974. For an explanation of the rapid growth of the SNP it is necessary to look to the failures of British governments rather than to allegations that they have discriminated against Scotland.

(3) The two aspects of national economic planning which have had most effect on Scotland are government policies regarding the location of industry and the financial management of the economy by the minimum lending rate, credit restrictions, tax changes and so forth. The first of these has benefited Scotland considerably, both through such measures as investment grants and investment allowances and through the control of industrial building. If Scotland had been independent in the past sixteen years it is unlikely that either Chrysler or British Leyland would have built factories there. London policies have also helped Scotland in relation to investment by overseas firms, and in 1969 a Scottish economist estimated that 'almost half the employment created by foreign firms since the war has gone to Scotland' (see McCrone, p. 75).

To say that Scotland has done relatively well out of British policies regarding the location of industry – probably better than Merseyside, for instance – is not to say that an independent Scotland could not have done better still. It rankles with Scottish nationalists that Scotland has to rely on the efforts of the Department of Trade and Industry in London to attract overseas investments while the Republic of Ireland has been able to develop its own very successful policies for this purpose and even the Northern Ireland administration has been able to open offices in foreign countries.

Another relevant economic argument is that the impact of government financial management on Scotland may not have been entirely beneficial. There have been times during the past twenty years when credit restrictions have been imposed to reduce demand in the English economy, when the Scottish economy needed a further increase in demand. It has also been said that Scottish industry needs lower interest rates (to encourage capital investment) than those fixed by the Bank of England to protect sterling. But these are rather technical arguments that are difficult to put to a mass electorate.

The Expectation of Economic or Diplomatic Advantages
None of the issues so far discussed can explain the phenomenal growth of Scottish nationalism in the past decade. The essential explanation of this is not to be found in any active sense that London governments have ill-treated Scotland, but in two other developments. The first of these is the inescapable evidence of mismanagement by London governments, leading to the belief that the Scots could govern themselves more efficiently and successfully than they have recently been governed by the English. The second – the 'eruptive factor' mentioned in Chapter 3 – is the discovery of North Sea oil.

That British governments have been unsuccessful in most of their major domestic policies since 1945 is now painfully obvious. That they have been particularly unsuccessful in economic management has been clear to economists for many years. There are numerous reasons for this and it would be wrong to ascribe the blame entirely to Westminster and Whitehall. But it is not surprising that ambitious people in the land that claims to be the birthplace of economic science should feel that they could do better by themselves.

Movements of support for nationalist objectives since 1945 have coincided with periods of obvious weakness in British economic management. The winter of 1946–7 first indicated to the British people that their wartime triumphs were to be followed by a painful rather than a triumphant peace. Food rationing in that period was more severe than it had been during the war, and gross mismanagement by the government led to a fuel crisis in January and February 1947 that caused nationwide power cuts and threw two million people out of work. In March 1947 a 'Scottish National Assembly' met in Glasgow to demand the establishment of a Scottish Parliament and within the next three years a Scottish Covenant pledging its signatories to this objective was signed by over a million people.

After 1951 Britain enjoyed a period of economic growth that continued until the credit squeeze of 1961. This boom was based on terms of trade that were in Britain's favour and it was said with some justice in the 1960s that the country had missed the opportunity to rebuild its industrial structure so as to be able to compete effectively when the trading position became more difficult. But for the British people these nine years brought a rapid improvement in the quality of their lives and a transformation of their expectations. Support for Scottish nationalism faded away, as did support for the Liberal Party in England. The Conservative Government achieved an unprecedented degree of success by increasing its majority at two successive general elections, and after the 1959 election it was seriously suggested that even the Labour Party might be condemned to an endless period of opposition (see, for instance, Abrams and Rose, *passim*; Mackintosh, p. 488).

However, the credit squeeze of 1961 dealt a serious blow to the hopes of a continuing and steady improvement in the standard of living; and 1961 was also the year in which British newspapers began to publish league tables showing that Britain was lagging behind other industrial nations in its rate of economic growth, in productivity per man, and in proportion of young people going on to higher education, particularly in science and technology. The Gallup Poll showed that in that year the Conservative Party lost the overall lead it had enjoyed since early 1958, not because of a swing to Labour but because of a swing to the smaller parties. Support for the Liberal Party increased from 6 per cent of the electorate in the last months of 1959 to 14 per cent in the last months of 1961, and early in 1962 the Liberals stunned political commentators by their by-election victory in the previously safe Conservative seat of Orpington.

In Scotland it was the SNP that gained rather than the Liberals. In November 1961 the SNP won 18 per cent of the votes at a by-election in Bridgeton and in June 1962 it won 23 per cent of the votes in West Lothian. In 1962 the SNP also established a widespread constituency organisation for the first time, and following this its membership increased from approximately 2,000 in 1962 to 55,000 in 1967. The electoral record of the party is shown in Table 6.2.

Table 6.2 *Electoral Record of the SNP*

General election	Candidates	Votes	Seats won
1959	5	21,738	—
1964	15	64,044	—
1966	23	128,474	—
1970	65	306,802	1
Feb. 1974	70	632,032	7
Oct. 1974	71	839,617	11

The proposition that the growth of the SNP owes a great deal to the failure of British governments in the economic field is supported by the electoral record of minor parties throughout Great Britain. In 1950 parties other than the two main parties gained 9·6 per cent of the total vote; in the 'never had it so good' election of 1959 the proportion fell to 6·6 per cent; in 1964 it rose to 12·3 per cent; in 1970 (when Britain enjoyed a healthy surplus on its current balance of payments) it slipped to 10·1 per cent; but by the crisis year of 1974 it had risen to 23·2 per cent in February and 23·0 per cent in October. The figures in Table 6.3 indicate that in the period of electoral breakthrough for the SNP, namely 1970–4, disenchantment with the two main parties actually grew more rapidly in England than in Scotland (or for that matter in Wales). But whereas disenchanted English voters had no choice but to emigrate or vote Liberal (which under the present electoral system brings them only a fraction of the influence to which they are numerically entitled), disenchanted Scottish voters could exercise more influence by supporting the SNP.

Table 6.3 *Proportion of Vote Cast for Minor Parties in 1970 and February 1974*

	1970 %	Feb. 1974 %	Increase %
England	8·0	22·1	176
Scotland	17·3	30·3	75
Wales	18·7	27·3	41

By couching the explanation in these terms it is not intended to imply that support for the SNP should be construed simply as a protest vote or a negative vote. The leaders and active members of the SNP are people of vision, imagination and determination. They believe that their country can be governed better by Scotsmen than it has been governed from London, and when the author attended their party's annual conference in 1975 he found that the most outstanding feature of the meeting was the confidence and optimism with which the delegates were imbued. It would be foolish to suppose that their supporters at the polls do not share this confidence. The point is simply that the party would not have achieved its dramatic successes since 1966 had it not been for the conspicuous failures of British economic management, which are recognised by voters south of the border just as clearly as they are by Scotsmen.

The other major factor in the growth of the SNP is of course the discovery of North Sea oil. Without this discovery, discontent with successive London governments would have been partially balanced by the fear that an independent Scotland would not be economically viable. These fears have been banished by the discovery of an oilfield off Scottish shores that by the early 1980s will be producing ten times as much oil as Scotland consumes. The SNP was quick to make political capital out of the economic possibilities opened up by this development, using effective propaganda slogans such as 'England Expects . . . Scotland's oil'. The details from a pamphlet with this title are worth quoting.

England expects Scottish oil to help pay for the third London airport and new city at Maplin (£2000m), the Channel Tunnel (£800m), a re-equipped Polaris submarine fleet (£1000m), the ever-rising Common Market levy and the colossal bill for Concorde. These projects damage the Scottish economy by concentrating even more jobs and prosperity in the south of England.

England expects the Scottish people to be grateful for handouts from London or Brussels when we could be the wealthiest nation in Europe if we controlled our own resources. Oil revenues alone, even on the minimum figure of £800 million per year, will be worth £3 per week for every man, woman and child in Scotland.

England expects Scotland to stand back and allow hasty uncontrolled exploitation of our oil in order to help the English balance of payments problem even if this causes unnecessary damage to local communities in the front line of the oil rush.

England expects Scottish public opinion to be bought off by a few oil refineries which bring only a sprinkling of jobs and which no other country wants because of the pollution and wastage of land.

Above all England expects that we the people of Scotland will sit back and allow our country to be exploited without taking action. The London establishment simply assumes that it has an absolute right to our wealth and resources without our consent and that, as always, the Scots will passively accept lower wages, higher prices, worse housing, more unemployment and high emigration. Let's prove them wrong.

The Character and Policies of the SNP

Nationalist movements of an aspiring kind are frequently touched with romanticism and influenced by the theorists and poets to be found among their leaders. They also tend to draw their activists from various strata of society, individuals linked by their devotion to a common cause rather than by common material interests. Thus, the Irish nationalist movement in the period 1914–16 had among its leaders such diverse types as Patrick Pearse – schoolteacher-poet; James Connolly – militant trade unionist; Eamonn de Valera – puritanical Catholic mathematician (half Irish, half Basque, born in New York); Countess Markievicz – revolutionary aristocrat; and Tom Clarke – shopkeeper and ex-convict.

Since 1946 the SNP has not conformed to this pattern at all. Its leaders have been practical men with respectable middle-class backgrounds whose appeals have been based on reason and self-interest rather than on rhetoric and poetic fervour. They have entirely rejected the emotional approach to political issues taken by such nationalists as Hugh MacDiarmid, the Marxist poet, and the Hon. Ruaraidh Erskine of Marr, who advocated a 'Celtic Renaissance' and thought it 'a child-like sort of faith' to believe 'in the possibility of destroying the English ascendancy in Scotland by sending members to the English Parliament' (quoted in Hanham, p. 145).

The long policy statement adopted by the SNP in December 1946 is a highly practical document, full of proposals about natural resources, agriculture, industry, housing and social security. The historian of Scottish nationalism has said that the most significant feature of this statement was 'the total omission of a section on Scottish culture' (see Hanham, p. 175). It took the existence of the Scottish nation for granted and set out the party's ideas on how the nation should be governed. The general tenor of the proposals was liberal, not socialist. Thus, the state should exercise 'an overriding control over the industrial structure of the country' through regional planning organisations but, subject to this control, private enterprise should be maintained and encouraged. Combines and monopolies should be prohibited and so should the closed shop. Agricultural co-operatives should be encouraged. The general spirit of the statements was nearer to that of the Liberal Party than to that of either of the two main parties, but with one important difference. Whereas Liberal Party statements of that period placed a good deal of emphasis on international affairs, the future of the Commonwealth and the hopes to be placed in the United Nations, the SNP statement was (apart from three sentences) entirely concerned with domestic affairs.

The leadership of the SNP today is solidly middle-class. All the members of the Executive Committee have middle-class occupations and so do the eleven Members of Parliament elected in 1974. The parliamentary group is comprised of four teachers, three businessmen, two lawyers, one journalist and a farmer. They were all educated at secondary day schools in Scotland and nine of them went to Scottish universities. In both their occupational and their educational backgrounds they therefore form a coherent group, to a much greater extent than Scottish Conservative or Labour MPs.

When the author attended the SNP annual conference in May 1975 he gained the impression that the delegates were drawn overwhelmingly from those groups in the community who rely on their own individual efforts rather than on inherited wealth or collective bargaining. The hall seemed to be full of engineers, computer operators, teachers, accountants and young business executives. There was not the mixture of accents, clothes and styles that are to be found at most party conferences, and neither was there such a wide spread of ages: at least 80 per cent of the delegates appeared to be between 25 and 45.

The mood of the conference was confident, practical and business-like. The speeches were good-humoured but not humorous, and the standard of logic during the debates was extraordinarily high. In two full days of discussion only one speaker digressed a little from the argument, and within thirty seconds he was interrupted by a point of order from the floor complaining about his lack of relevance. There was no rhetoric about Scotland's illustrious past and distinctive culture; there was no waving of banners or playing of bagpipes; and there was no trace of animosity towards the English.

The policy of the SNP towards the constitutional issue is straightforward. The party believes that if it won a majority of the 71 Scottish seats in the House of Commons this victory would give it a mandate to treat for independence. It would expect to enter into detailed negotiations with the UK government about the transfer of power, the status of civil servants, the division of the national debt, and similar issues. It would then propose that the 71 Scottish MPs should constitute the first Scottish Parliament, to draw up a constitution and make arrangements for the first general election in the new state. The SNP does not apparently have any contingency plans to meet the possibility that the UK government might refuse to grant independence in these circumstances, as its public position is that such behaviour would be unthinkable.

As already noted, the SNP does not simply rest its case on the arguments for Scottish independence and the means by which this can be attained. Ever since 1946, the greater part of its policy statements have been devoted to the domestic issues that a Scottish government would face. In the manifesto for the October 1974 election only 20 per cent of the space (as measured in column inches) was devoted to the case for independence, the history of the party and the constitutional issue. A further 10 per cent of the manifesto was devoted to the policies towards external affairs and defence that the SNP advocated for an independent Scotland, 14 per cent to policies regarding oil and other energy resources, and the remaining 56 per cent to domestic issues such as housing, agriculture, pensions and economic development. This readiness to be judged on the policies it would promote after independence distinguishes the SNP from most other nationalist movements of the past hundred years, which have usually directed a high proportion of their propaganda to emphasising the value of their country's culture and the iniquitous nature of its treatment under the existing system. In May 1974 the Secretary of State for Scotland chose to describe the SNP in a televised speech as 'that shoddy party that disgraces the name of Scotland with its cheap slogans that divide the nation'. No impartial observer could possibly accept this as a fair judgement. Whatever its failings, the SNP must be rated as one of the most constructive nationalist parties the world has seen.

The detailed policies of the SNP put it somewhere in the centre of the political spectrum. Because it did not take sides in the trade unions' conflict with the Conservative Government, and does not believe in nationalisation for ideological motives, it has often been criticised by Labour supporters as being a party of 'Tartan Tories'. Some support for this assessment can be found in the evident enthusiasm of the 1975 conference for resolutions favouring the self-employed and in the fact that the conference defeated the only resolution proposed by the Association of Scottish Nationalist Trade Unionists. This resolution called for the immediate reintroduction of flat-rate threshold payments to meet rises in the cost of living, and it was defeated on the ground that it would be unfair to higher-paid workers, would be inflationary, and would cause cash-flow problems for firms who could not raise their prices.

However, in many respects the SNP's policies are quite different from those of the Conservative Party. For instance, it believes that 'ultimately the land belongs to the people' and has proposed the creation of a Land Use Commission which could compel landowners to develop their land 'in ways most appropriate for the benefit of the local community or of the nation'. It has come out in favour of industrial democracy and profit-sharing. It has proposed larger increases in pensions and certain other welfare benefits. It would close down all nuclear bases in Scotland and has always been opposed to British (or Scottish) membership of the EEC. (Quotations from *Scotland's Future*, the manifesto issued in August 1974.) As suggested earlier, the SNP's domestic policies are nearer to those of the Liberal Party than to either of the major parties, though it does not share the Liberals' idealistic commitments to such issues as the continuance of Commonwealth immigration.

The Prospects for Scottish Nationalism
It is appropriate to consider this question under two headings, one with a narrow and the other with a broader perspective. The first is the short-term prospect for the electoral success of the SNP and the second is the wider question of the movements of opinion in both Scotland and England about the future of Scottish governments.

There are two reasons for expecting that the SNP might improve its position significantly at the next general election. The first is the astonishing growth in the electoral popularity of the party since 1970. A party which has almost trebled its share of the poll in four years may be assumed to have a good chance of improving its position further unless the political situation has changed markedly to its disadvantage, either as a result of its own behaviour or because one of the older parties has succeeded in alleviating the discontent which led to the growth of the younger party. The second reason is the failure of the Labour Government in London to deal successfully with the economic crisis. Between October 1974 and October 1976 inflation continued at a much higher rate than Britain had ever experienced before 1974; the value of the pound fell from $2·30 to $1·60; unemployment rose sharply; and the government was forced to admit that real incomes were going to fall in 1977 and not recover for some time to come. In as far as the economic failures of London governments were a major reason for the growth of the SNP up to October 1974, it might be expected that the even more serious failures since 1974 would enable the SNP to make spectacular gains at the next general election.

However, recent public opinion polls give little support to such an expectation. In the autumn of 1976 two polls indicated that it was the Conservative Party rather than the SNP that had gained from the failures of the Labour Government and the increasing evidence of ideological cleavages within the Labour Party (see *The Scotsman*, 29 October 1976 and 11 November 1976). One possible explanation of this is that the bitter political clashes at Westminster may have tended to reinforce ideological and class divisions, with critics of the Labour Party turning (or returning) to the Conservatives as Labour's most effective opponents. Another possible explanation is that support for Scottish nationalism may have reached a plateau in 1974.

One fact that points towards the second explanation is the apparent inability of the SNP to match its electoral success by large-scale conversions to the cause of Scottish independence. Repeated public opinion polls on this subject have shown that the proportion of voters willing to support this objective varies between 17 per cent and 21 per cent, the exact figure within this range depending largely on the way the question is worded (see, for instance, the polls reported in *The Economist*, 18 May 1974, and *The Scotsman*, 26 October 1976). With four-fifths of the Scottish people apparently committed to the maintenance of the United Kingdom, it seems reasonable to argue that the future prospects of the nationalist movement depend less on the behaviour of the SNP than on the reactions of the United Kingdom parties to the widespread demand for a measure of political devolution. These reactions will be examined in Chapter 9.

7

Welsh Nationalism

Welsh nationalism is in some ways a more complex phenomenon than Scottish nationalism. On the one hand, the Welsh sense of national consciousness is less secure than the equivalent Scottish sense and in a variety of ways – many of which have been discussed in Chapters 2 and 3 – Wales is much more closely integrated with England than Scotland is. On the other hand, the resentment of English dominance that is to be found in some sections of Welsh society has a longer history and is a good deal stronger than any Scottish equivalent.

The existence of a certain ambiguity about the right of Wales to be described as a nation is not surprising in view of the country's history. Wales has never had a unified government of its own and from the sixteenth century until the twentieth century there were no distinctively Welsh political institutions apart from the Council of Wales, which met in England and was abolished in 1689. Welsh customary law was replaced by English law, the Church of England was the established church, local authorities and state schools were organised in the same way throughout Wales and England. Moreover, the cohesion of Welsh society was weakened from the sixteenth century onwards by the Anglicisation of the land-owning and educated classes, so that the bulk of the Welsh people were separated from their natural leaders by linguistic, cultural and (later) religious divisions. It has been said that the position in Wales came to resemble that in Ireland, 'except that the Welsh gentry were of the same race as their tenantry whereas in Ireland they were of English descent' (D. Williams, p. 89).

In the nineteenth century the industrialisation of South Wales carried the process of Anglicisation very much farther. The development of Welsh industry depended upon English capital to a greater extent than had the development of Scottish industry and was accompanied by the migration to South Wales of English managers, engineers and manual workers (including miners from Devon and Cornwall). The 1881 census showed that 15 per cent of the population of Wales had been born in England, and the proportion rose to 19 per cent in 1891 and 22 per cent in 1911. In the industrial areas of South Wales the proportions were appreciably higher.

The 1846 report on Welsh education had already persuaded the British government of the desirability of discouraging the use of the Welsh language, on the ground that 'because of their language, the mass of the Welsh people are inferior to the English in every branch of practical knowledge and skill' (quoted in Hechter, p. 75). The 1870 Education Act provided that all teaching had to be conducted in English and it also banned the teaching of Welsh in grant-aided schools. This ban only lasted until 1889, when it was agreed that Welsh could be taught as a foreign language on an equal basis with other foreign languages. But the combination of this educational policy with the impact of industrial and commercial developments had the inevitable effect of turning Wales into a predominantly English-speaking country. Census figures show that 50 per cent of the population still claimed knowledge of Welsh in 1901, but this was an overall figure and the proportion in Cardiff was only 8·2 per cent. The national proportions fell to 37 per cent in 1931 and 21 per cent in 1971, with all but 1 per cent being able to speak English as well. Most of those who can speak Welsh live in the rural areas of the north and west.

It follows that language can no longer serve as a basis for national self-consciousness, except among a rather small minority. Other aspects of the traditional way of life, such as Nonconformity and teetotalism, have also lost a good deal of their significance with the decline of religious observance. The geography of Wales hardly binds the country together, and the circulation of the only Welsh morning newspaper (95,000) is small compared with the Welsh circulation of the London morning papers (over 600,000). It would be wrong to ignore the strong sense of community that exists in urban as well as rural areas of Wales, or certain cultural traits – such as an egalitarian tradition, a deep concern for education, and a widespread love of music – that make Welsh social values rather different from their English equivalents. Nevertheless, a degree of ambiguity about Welsh national identity is indicated by the prevalence of such expressions as 'very Welsh' and 'Welsh Wales', which have no Scottish equivalents. There appears to be a dimension of Welshness, and it is the realisation that much of Welsh society has been moving away from the truly Welsh end of this dimension that is responsible for a good deal of the passion that has motivated Welsh nationalists in recent years. As the president of Plaid Cymru and one of his colleagues wrote in 1968: 'We Welsh are not just being denied self-expression as a nation today. . . . We are fighting in the last ditch for our very identity' (Edwards *et al.*, p. 259).

Political activities designed to secure special laws for Wales have a fairly long history. In the last two decades of the nineteenth century Welsh politicians were struggling for the disestablishment of the Church of England in Wales, for a ban on the Sunday opening of public houses, for land reforms, and for the improvement of Welsh education (for details, see Morgan). But I am concerned in this chapter with nationalism, defined as a demand for self-government rather than for reform, and this emerged in 1932 when Plaid Cymru (the Welsh Party, founded in 1925 to defend and promote the Welsh language) adopted self-government as a necessary political means to this end. The factors underlying the development and recent growth of this movement will be examined under the same headings as those used for Scottish nationalism.

Cultural Domination

Whereas resentment of cultural domination by the English is unimportant in Scotland, it is the mainspring of modern Welsh nationalism. In the absence of an institutional basis for Welsh nationhood, nationalist thinkers have long regarded their language as essential to the preservation of their society. As long ago as 1833, the journal *Y Cymmro* declared in an editorial:

> If once we lose the Welsh language, that will be the end of us as a nation; the sun of the Welsh people will set, never to rise again; and they will not be heard of any more as a nation but merely as a piece of driftwood that has survived from a wreck that disappeared in the great ocean of oblivion. (Quoted in Tudor Jones, p. 134.)

In 1907 Emrys ap Iwan expressed the same view in an even more apocalyptic mood:

> Let it be remembered that the God who made men ordained nations also; and to exterminate a nation is a tragedy next in seriousness to exterminating humanity, and to exterminate a nation's language is the tragedy next in seriousness to exterminating a nation, because a nation ceases to be a nation sooner or later after losing its language. (Quoted in Tudor Jones, p. 185.)

Modern nationalists do not leave the argument in quite such a stark form, but argue that the decline of the language is also depriving the Welsh people of a literary heritage and a traditional folk-culture of songs and verse. The leaders of the nationalist movement are old-fashioned in the sense that they believe people are likely to get more happiness from making their own music than from watching television. They are concerned also about the decline of religion and the growth of materialism. A study of local voting on the prohibition of liquor sales on Sundays – said to be an important symbol of the traditional Welsh way of life – showed a significant decline between 1961 and 1968, with the 'drys' holding only the 'core areas' of the Welsh culture. The authors predicted progressive Anglicisation leading to eventual disintegration of even the core areas (see Carter and Thomas).

The penetration and erosion of one culture by another often stimulate political activity of a defensive kind. The increased penetration of Quebec by Anglo-American culture has been accompanied by an increase in French-Canadian nationalism, and the recent growth of Welsh nationalism is essentially a re-action by groups who see their culture threatened with extinction. It can also be argued that it is a sense of desperation, produced by this threat, which has led some Welsh nationalists (unlike Scottish nationalists) to advocate direct action and even political violence. Thus Saunders Lewis, the main philosopher of Welsh nationalism, has said this in an interview:

> I personally believe that careful, considered public violence is often a necessary weapon for national movements, necessary to defend the land, the valleys of Wales from being violated . . . by the government and by the big corporations in England. (Quoted in Thomas, p. 62.)

Since the 1920s the most important motivating force of the nationalist groups has been their concern to arrest the decline of the Welsh language. This struggle has been waged with considerable vigour in recent years, not only by Plaid Cymru but also by the more militant Welsh Language Society (founded in 1962), whose members have resorted to direct action on numerous occasions. The majority of the Welsh people have viewed the struggle with either apathy or hostility, as Saunders Lewis deplored in his 1962 lecture on 'The Fate of the Language'. But the impact of nationalist groups on the decisions of the British government has been considerable in spite of the numerical weakness of the groups. As Saunders Lewis observed, 'the

Ministry of Education fosters the Welsh language and urges it on the schools more earnestly than the Welsh local authorities' (see Jones and Thomas, pp. 127–8). Welsh can be used in the courts and in applications to some government departments, and the language is now advertised on bilingual road signs throughout Wales.

It is unlikely that these developments will reverse the decline of the language, though they may of course retard it. The difficulties in the way of turning Wales into a fully bilingual country are insuperable in an interdependent world in which the mass media play such an important role. The experience of the Irish Republic is clear evidence of this. If the real aim of Welsh nationalists is not to make Wales a bilingual country but merely to prevent the death of the Welsh language, the Irish experience will not discourage them. However, the emphasis given to the language issue by the nationalists is a political handicap to Plaid Cymru in the English-speaking areas.

As noted, it is not only the linguistic issue that leads Welsh nationalists to resent the cultural domination of the English in their country. They dislike the materialism of modern English life and what they see as its lack of spiritual values. Sometimes these feelings are expressed in terms which the English find difficult to understand. Some of their publications are written in a rather romantic style, and at the end of the verbal evidence given by the leaders of Plaid Cymru to the Commission on the Constitution the chairman of the Commission observed that he found it hard to attach a precise meaning to many of the points that had been made. But it should not be impossible to understand the essence of the Welsh nationalists' dream of a simpler life, with closer community relationships and more emphasis on personal creative activities than on watching mass-produced entertainments.

Political Discrimination
Like Scotland, Wales is over-represented in the House of Commons, though not to the same extent. It has 36 seats instead of the 31 it would have if it were represented equally with England. However, Welsh nationalists have a different kind of complaint about the British political system. Unlike the Scots, they believe passionately that democracy in Britain (as in many other modern states) is seriously threatened by the centralisation of the system and the size of the bureaucracy. It is perhaps best to quote Gwynfor Evans on this topic:

The residue of democratic control even in English national and local life is being continuously eroded. . . . Amongst individual persons and local communities freedom and power to fashion their environment decreases; while central governments, one after another, pursue policies contrary to the election prospectus they had published, regardless of the opinion of the electors, who cannot influence them by parliamentary and democratic means. The logic of this increasing centralism is totalitarianism. The resuscitation of the English democracy requires radical decentralisation of power to English regional governments, just as the creation of a Welsh democracy demands decentralisation of power to Wales. (Evans (*a*), pp. 100–1.)

Economic Domination
Welsh nationalists are not as concerned about economic issues as the SNP, except in one respect. This is the threat to the employment situation posed by the plans to shut down a large part of the Welsh steel industry and the longer-term probability of pit closures. Nationalist leaders are reluctant to accept the British Steel Corporation's argument that only giant steel plants can now be economic. They suspect that this is a further example of the passion for centralisation which they deplore. Moreover, this is an issue on which Plaid Cymru can expect to gain support in the English-speaking areas. The strength of community spirit among Welsh workers makes them less willing than English workers are to move to another area in search of work – and particularly unwilling to move to England. The government's policy in the 1930s of offering financial assistance to unemployed workers in the depressed areas of Britain if they had to move home to secure a job has been described by the president of Plaid Cymru as a 'barbarous policy of transference which uprooted the people of Wales from local community and from country, from culture and language, from choir and chapel, friends and society' (Evans (*c*), p. 12).

It is not at all clear that a Welsh government could improve the prospects of the Welsh steel and coal industries without subsidies from English taxpayers. Welsh coal is now very expensive and in strictly economic terms it might well be cheaper for England to import coal from Poland or the United States. But Plaid Cymru does not aim to do without assistance from English taxpayers, as its policy is not 'independence' but 'self-government'. The theory is that each nation within the British Isles should be autonomous in economic planning but should co-operate with its neighbours in a friendly and constructive way. In practice, this means that the Welsh would expect the English to go on buying Welsh coal in preference to Polish or American coal, whether or not it was the best buy from the English point of view. If a hard-headed English government were disinclined to subsidise the Welsh mining industry in this way, pressure might well be exerted on it – if Wales were self-governing – by a threat to cut off the water from Welsh reservoirs on which Liverpool and Birmingham now depend.

The Expectation of Economic or Diplomatic Advantage
In the 1974 elections Plaid Cymru borrowed slogans from the SNP, with whom it maintains fairly close links, and the February 1974 manifesto of the Plaid was entitled *Rich Welsh or Poor British*. But it differs from the SNP in stressing that the main advantage of self-government would be greater democracy rather than greater efficiency. In so far as the Welsh nationalists claim that there would be economic advantages in self-government, the claim rests on the hopes that: (1) they would be able to levy a charge on water supplies from Welsh reservoirs to English cities; (2) if and when oil is discovered under the Celtic Sea, Wales would get the benefit; and (3) the achievement of self-government would generate a burst of enthusiasm and energy that would revitalise the economy.

If this prospectus for economic growth does not seem very plausible, the reason is not only that as yet Wales lacks any equivalent of North Sea oil but also that the leaders of Plaid Cymru are not basically interested in economic growth. Their concern is for language, culture and the quality of life, and their president indicated in 1975 that he was glad that there would be no oil from the Celtic Sea for at least a decade (Evans (c), p. 113).

Of course, Welsh electors have not escaped the disenchantment with the two main parties that has affected other British electors in recent years, though the figures given on page 109 suggest that it has been smaller in scale. However, disenchanted Welsh electors, like English electors, have turned to the Liberal Party to register their protest. Between the elections of 1970 and October 1974 the Liberal vote increased from 103,747 to 238,997 while that of Plaid Cymru declined from 175,016 to 166,321. These figures suggest that the Blaid is still seen as a party of cultural distinctiveness and has not been able to derive much benefit from the general economic and political discontents affecting the Welsh people. Details of its electoral record since 1951 are given in Table 7.1, from which it will be seen that Plaid Cymru had wider support than the SNP until 1964 but has not been able to match the meteoric growth of SNP support since that year.

Table 7.1 *Nationalist Votes at General Elections: 1951–74*

Election	Plaid Cymru			SNP		
	Candidates	Votes	Seats won	Candidates	Votes	Seats won
1951	4	10,920	—	2	7,299	—
1955	11	45,119	—	2	12,112	—
1959	20	77,571	—	5	21,738	—
1964	23	69,507	—	15	64,044	—
1966	20	61,071	—	23	128,474	—
1970	36	175,016	—	65	306,802	1
Feb. 1974	36	171,364	2	70	632,032	7
Oct. 1974	36	166,321	3	71	839,617	11

The Philosophy of the Welsh Nationalists

Plaid Cymru is in some ways a more typical nationalist party than the SNP. Like the Irish, Basque, Breton and Quebecois nationalist movements, the Welsh nationalists are politicians with a grievance concerned to assert and defend the cultural identity of their nation. They are more visionary and less pragmatic than the Scots, and much more given to expressing themselves in a poetical and rhetorical fashion.

It must be said that the rhetoric of Welsh nationalists occasionally has mystical overtones that are rather bewildering to outsiders. An early statement of Welsh nationalist aims, published in 1913, began its concluding paragraph in the following manner:

And beyond that – let us repeat it – we dare to dream of the time when the nation itself shall be a church – when labour shall be known as holy service, when democracy shall be a priesthood, when workshop and cottage, senate and mart, shall be sanctuaries of the Eternal. (Griffith, p. 92.)

When the Air Ministry decided to establish a bombing range in an uninhabited stretch of Welsh countryside in 1936 Saunders Lewis (then president of Plaid Cymru) was so outraged that he set fire to the buildings, for which he subsequently went to prison. In a prepared statement at his trial he said he had done this to 'protest on behalf of the truly sacred things in Creation – the nation, its language, its literature, its separate traditions and immemorial ways of Christian life' (Jones and Thomas, p. 122). Commenting on this in 1968, Gwynfor Evans and Ioan Rhys said that the range was sited 'in unspoilt country steeped in history and evocative of all the simplicity of the Celtic Saints' (Edwards *et al.*, p. 256).

This kind of statement is almost incomprehensible to the pragmatic English, or for that matter to the Lowland Scots. What is more comprehensible, but rarely understood, is the extent to which Welsh nationalists are committed to particular communities and a particular way of life within Wales. Thus, following numerous complaints that the rural areas of central Wales were suffering from depopulation, English town planners thought they would get a friendly welcome for their proposal to build a new town in the area to rehouse people from Birmingham. To their astonishment, they were immediately accused by Plaid Cymru spokesmen of a plot to commit genocide. It was said in speeches and articles, and has been explained to me in an interview, that a plan to deposit 50,000 English people in an area that was still predominantly Welsh-speaking could only be regarded as a plot to destroy Welsh culture in that part of the country. The opposition was so vehement that the plan was eventually abandoned, even though it had had the support of the Welsh Office when it was launched.

An even more vigorous campaign was waged against the Private Bill tabled in 1955 to authorise the Liverpool City Council to flood the Tryweryn valley in the course of constructing a reservoir to augment Liverpool's water supplies. There were demonstrations and arguments which continued for over twelve months before Parliament eventually agreed to the Liverpool plan. It did so largely on the ground that the reservoir would involve the rehousing of only 70 families, which is a relatively small number to make way for a large reservoir in a crowded country like Britain. It may be asked why the Welsh nationalists were so passionately concerned about this project when the number of people involved was so small. The answer, as given to me by Gwynfor Evans, is that the displaced families were Welsh-speaking. He agreed that if they had been English-speaking Welshmen he and his colleagues would not have minded quite so much.

This is an unusual but entirely consistent political viewpoint which ascribes more importance to some citizens than to others on the ground of the language they speak. It was reflected again in the comment Gwynfor Evans and Ioan Rhys made on the refusal of the Board of Trade to schedule certain quarrying districts of North Wales as a development area, because the number of unemployed persons there was 'not significant in the national total'. Their comment was that 'the numerical strength of the districts concerned bore little relation to their significance in Welsh life . . . it was these areas which had been producing a crop of writers unequalled in the Welsh language since the fifteenth century' (Edwards *et al.*, pp. 259–60). Evans' attitude towards the impact of Anglicisation is encapsulated in his remark: 'The language of getting on in the world is now the only tongue of three-quarters of the people of Wales. Barbarism has many faces' (Evans (*b*), p. 9).

This attitude towards politics implies a rejection of the view that the interests of the majority should necessarily prevail in cases of dispute. The leaders of the Welsh nationalist movement are entirely consistent about this. They believe that where there is a conflict between the interests of a local community and those of a numerical majority, the local interest should normally have priority. They envisage that a self-governing Wales would have a decentralised system of government. They favour co-operative and workers' control in nationalised industries, and prefer 'Proudhon and William Morris to both Marx and the Webbs' (Edwards *et al.*, p. 258).

In Plaid Cymru manifestoes and pamphlets the aim of the party is always described as 'self-government' or 'freedom', never as 'independence'. This distinction was first formulated by Saunders Lewis, who wrote as follows in his 1926 pamphlet on *The Principles of Nationalism*:

> First of all, let us not ask for independence for Wales. Not because it is impracticable, but because it is not worth having . . . it is materialistic and cruel, leading to violence, oppression and ideas already proved to be bad. . . . So let us insist on having, not independence, but freedom. (S. Lewis, p. 9.)

Later in the same pamphlet he concluded:

> We must have self-government. Not independence. Not even unconditional freedom. But just as much freedom as may be necessary to establish and safeguard civilisation in Wales.

The philosophy underlying these statements is important to Welsh nationalists and is frequently reiterated by them, and it is surprising to find no discussion of it in the academic lierature on the subject.

What is the character of the political philosophy that has inspired Plaid Cymru? Basically, it rests on an idealisation of the political system of medieval Europe, before the continent was divided into sovereign nation-states. Saunders Lewis wrote in the pamphlet already quoted that in medieval times

> There was one law and one civilisation throughout Europe; but that law, that civilisation took on many forms and many colours. It did not occur to the rulers of a country to destroy the characteristics of another land's civilisation even when they conquered that land.

The social order depended on the acceptance of a common moral law, but was not thought to be threatened by the co-existence of a wide variety of languages and local cultures. Hence it was that the Welsh heritage was not in danger in medieval times, even though Wales had been conquered. But when the modern nation-state developed in the sixteenth century the rulers of England began their long campaign to destroy Welsh civilisation in the course of establishing the political unity of the kingdom, now separated from Europe and hostile to it. Lewis summarised his attitude to Welsh nationalism in the following words:

> What, then, is our nationalism? This; a return to the medieval principle; a denial of the benefits of political uniformity, and a demonstration of its ill-effects; thereby arguing in favour of the principle of unity and variety. Not a fight for Wales' independence but for Wales' civilisation. . . . A claim that she should have a seat in the Society of Nations and European society by virtue of the value of her civilisation.

Of course, not all the leaders of the Welsh nationalist movement look back so specifically to the Middle Ages. But they all dislike the nineteenth- and early twentieth-century idea that the world should be divided into sovereign, independent nation-states. Their conception of the ideal political order is that it should be a community of communities, linked inevitably in a kind of geographical hierarchy, but without the means for one community to impose its will on another. It is this political ideal which underlies Plaid Cymru's proposal that a self-governing Wales should be linked with the other nations of the British Isles in a Britannic Confederation, whose activities would evolve as a consequence of the partnership between its members. Equally, it is this view which explains the somewhat ambivalent attitude Plaid Cymru has taken towards the EEC over the years, which can be summarised with only a modicum of unfairness by saying that it has favoured the idea of the EEC in so far as it looked like becoming a community without a clear process of decision-making, but has been against it in so far as it threatens (as it now does) to become a supranational bureaucracy, or to erect military or economic barriers between itself and the rest of the world.

It is clear from this analysis that the philosophy of the Welsh nationalist movement is very different from that of contemporary Scottish nationalism. The Scots are business-like and progressive and claim that they could run an industrial society more efficiently than it is run under present management. The Welsh are visionary and romantic and essentially hostile to the values associated with an industrial society. Equally, while SNP leaders believe in individualism, the Welsh leaders regard the community as the basic unit of social life. In an attack on both the impact of industrialisation and the ideals of the Manchester School, a former acting president of the Blaid declared that industrial capitalism 'ignores all the things that make of man something more than an animated tool, the things that make him a person – family, nation, religion' (Daniel, p. 21). The current president also likes the term 'person' and has said that 'the individual does not exist . . . a person is a social being integrated in society and made what he is by that society' (Evans (b), p. 10).

The idealism of the Welsh nationalists is shown by their constant concern for the position of other minority groups whom they consider to be oppressed. Plaid Cymru is affiliated to the Bureau of Unrepresented European Nations, together with representatives of Alsace-Lorraine, Brittany and the Basque country. In October 1975 the three Plaid Cymru MPs protested against the execution of five Basque nationalists in Spain and called for the severance of diplomatic relations between Spain and the United Kingdom. The party's journal, *Welsh Nation*, features frequent articles drawing attention to French ill-treatment of Breton and Corsican nationalists, and has commented on the happier lot of national minorities in Yugoslavia. Plaid Cymru is the only party represented in Parliament to show sympathy for Iceland during the Cod War, the *Welsh Nation* saying in a front-page editorial that the British Government was 'using the Royal Navy to bully the Iceland Government, anxious to prevent its one natural resource from being fished out of existence' (*Welsh Nation*, 12–18 March 1976). Equally, the paper was the only paper in Britain to celebrate the centenary of the foundation of the Genootskap van Regte Afrikaners – the Society of True Afrikaners – which was established in 1875 to promote the Afrikaans language. In a comment that readers of any other British journal in 1975 would have found incredible, it was said that the founders 'braved abuse and persecution to give their homespun language a new strength, beauty and dignity. They were right to persist. The world honours them today' (*Welsh Nation*, 5–11 December 1975).

In the methods adopted to secure their objectives, the Welsh nationalists are more varied than the Scots. Whereas the latter have confined themselves to the normal types of propaganda and to contesting elections, Welsh nationalists have also engaged in non-violent forms of direct action. With the tacit approval of Plaid Cymru, the Welsh Laguage Society has been willing to flout the law in its campaigns to secure equality of status between Welsh and English. Since 1965 over five hundred of the Society's members have been imprisoned for such offences as defacing road signs, refusing to comply with regulations (such as licensing their cars) because the official forms were available only in English, refusing to pay fines, and holding 'sit-ins' in BBC studios. There has been no violence except by one tiny group, and the temper of the movement is essentially non-violent. But a new and more extreme organisation called Adfer has been established in the 1970s, whose members even paint out the English directions on bilingual road signs, and passions run so high among a small minority of nationalists that it would be foolish to rule out the possibility that violent conflicts may develop in the future.

The Membership and Policies of Plaid Cymru

The size and composition of the membership of Plaid Cymru has been subjected to an exhaustive analysis by Alan Butt Philip, who wrote a D.Phil. thesis on the topic. Unfortunately the official figures that he quotes are mutually inconsistent and bewildering in their variety. It seems clear that the party had only a small membership until the mid-sixties, but that it increased rapidly during the late sixties. The annual reports of Plaid Cymru quoted membership figures of 3,475 in 1965, 16,000 in 1966, 27,000 in 1967, and 40,000 in 1968. Party officials estimated the 1969 membership to be 42,000 but as a result of a detailed scrutiny of constituency reports Philip produced his own estimate for 1969 of only 19,000 paid-up members (see Philip, p. 171).

The discrepancy arose largely from the habit of constituency branches of keeping people on the books once they had joined, whether or not they paid any further subscriptions. In November 1976, the general secretary of the party told me that the best estimate he could make of the total membership was between 30,000 and 35,000. In view of Philip's figures, it is not certain whether this represents an increase or a decrease since 1969, but I think it probably represents an increase as the party's organisation has improved and it now employs six full-time local organisers as well as the head-office staff. In comparison, the SNP claimed a membership of about 75,000 in 1976.

Not surprisingly, all the leaders and parliamentary candidates have been drawn from middle-class occupations. The teaching profession has contributed more than any other. Half of the fifty-seven individuals who contested parliamentary elections between 1945 and 1966 were teachers or lecturers, as were at least twelve of the twenty members of the 1969 Executive (see Philip, pp. 155–6). However, the party's dependence on teachers is declining as it broadens its social basis: the number of teachers or lecturers among the thirty-six parliamentary candidates fell from fifteen in 1970 to thirteen in February 1974 and eleven in October 1974. The other candidates in the last election included five lawyers, four engineers or scientists, four local government officials, a psychiatrist, a folk-singer and an actress. It is characteristic of the Blaid that one of the four businessmen who stood describes himself in *The Times House of Commons* not only as a 'construction executive' but also as a 'poet, lyricist and member of the International Songwriters' Association'.

Although the Blaid's expansion since 1965 does not compare with the SNP's expansion in electoral terms, it has become much more widely based. In 1965 the heart of the party was in the rural areas of north and west Wales, where its activists were almost entirely Welsh-speaking. By 1976 the party had thriving branches throughout the industrial areas of south-east Wales, many of whose members did not speak Welsh. In the October 1974 election Plaid Cymru candidates in the nineteen constituencies of south-east Wales secured a total of 64,981 votes, an average of 3,420 each, while candidates in the seventeen other constituencies secured 101,340 votes, an average of 5,961 each. A comparison of these results with those of the 1964 election discloses an increase in the total Blaid vote of 173 per cent in south-east Wales and an increase of 121 per cent in the rest of the country. Though still a very small party, the Blaid has now established itself in all areas of Wales, and surveys suggest that it draws its electoral support from all occupational groups in rough proportion to the overall size of each group (see Philip, pp. 150–1).

The policies of a party inevitably reflect its composition. As the Blaid has broadened its base, it has somewhat moderated its stand on the language issue. Its original objective was an all Welsh-speaking Wales, but by the 1950s party spokesmen were talking of a bilingual Wales as the aim. It was not until the 1969 conference, however, that the party officially indicated that a bilingual nation was its objective (see Philip, p. 117). As the party has grown, it has also become slightly more realistic about the pace of the change that might be expected; for instance, it is prepared to accept that it would take some years before all the public officials in the country could speak Welsh. However, it should not be thought that the Blaid is likely to become 'realistic' about the language issue in the full meaning of that term. Its older leaders, including the president, Gwynfor Evans, and the vice-president, Robyn Lewis, are completely dedicated to the revival of the language. Many of its young recruits come into the party by way of Welsh youth movements that are language-oriented. If the Blaid were to compromise its position on the language it would risk losing many of its most active and energetic members to the Welsh Language Society or to the more militant organisation called Adfer. In a real sense, the Welsh language is still what Plaid Cymru is mainly about.

It has other policies, however, and since 1966 these have mostly been addressed to the economic problems of Wales, which are even more serious than those of England. These policies are left-wing, not because there is any necessary connection between nationalism and socialism but because the political centre of gravity of Wales is considerably further to the left than that of England, Scotland or Ireland. The Conservative Party has never been strong there since 1868 and in the later nineteenth century Wales was a Liberal stronghold. In the four general elections between 1900 and 1910 the Liberals never won less than 26 of the 34 Welsh seats and after the First World War they were replaced by the Labour Party, which has won a majority of Welsh seats in every election since 1922. In the seven elections between 1950 and 1970 Labour never won fewer than 27 of the 36 Welsh seats. In view of this radical tradition it is not surprising that the Blaid's economic policies are considerably more left-wing than those of the SNP.

It is perhaps surprising, however, that in many respects the Blaid's policies are more radical than those of the Labour Party. The 1974 manifesto called for the municipalisation of private rented property and holiday homes; for greater equality of earnings; for an expansion of social services; and for ownership of all but the smallest business concerns to be vested in the hands of their workers with 'each employee having equal rights'. It would seem that in terms of electoral strategy, the Blaid has committed itself to the aim of attracting support from Labour voters rather than to the SNP's strategy of attracting support from all parts of the political spectrum.

The Prospects for Welsh Nationalism

If this question is viewed narrowly in terms of the electoral prospects for Plaid Cymru, it is difficult to find grounds for predicting rapid growth. The party's candidates secured only 10·8 per cent of the Welsh vote in October 1974 and none of the thirty-three unsuccessful candidates got more than a quarter of the votes in his constituency. Unlike the SNP, the Blaid would need an enormous swing in its favour to win any extra seats at the next election.

If the question is viewed in broader terms, it becomes rather complicated. On the one hand, the commitment of the nationalists to the Welsh language is a serious obstacle in their efforts to gain support from the non-Welsh-speaking majority. It is intrinsically difficult to persuade people who do not speak Welsh to support a movement which wants to force them and their children to learn the language, and to give priority to Welsh-speakers in appointments to local government, the teaching profession and the civil service. Surveys show that less than a third of Welsh people support the view that Welsh should be made a compulsory subject in all Welsh schools (see Commission on the Constitution, Research Paper 7, p. 15.)

Moreover, statistical projections make the whole issue look like a lost cause. The 1970 survey for the Commission on the Constitution reported a clear decline among younger people, with only 13 per cent of respondents under forty claiming to speak the language (Research Paper 7, p. 56). A professor of modern languages has concluded, with regret, that 'the outlook must be bleak' (Lockwood, p. 33). If Gwynfor Evans and his colleagues are correct in their assumption that the language is the only possible basis of Welsh nationhood, and if linguists and statisticians are right in their belief that the language is bound to decline, it would seem logical to conclude that the nationalist movement is itself likely to be only a temporary phenomenon.

This deduction is logically incontrovertible provided the premises are correct. However, both the premises are matters of dispute. The inevitability of the decline of the language is rejected not only by Plaid Cymru leaders but also by an influential language lobby, some of whose members vote for other parties. An interesting example is the Gittins Report on *Primary Education in Wales*, a massive document of over 600 pages that was prepared for the Department of Education and Science by the Central Advisory Council for Education (Wales). The nineteen members of this Council (who were appointed by the Secretary of State) include a clear majority of Welsh-speakers, so that in this respect the Council is significantly unrepresentative of the Welsh population. The only social scientist on the Council has said that he 'was surprised to find that at the first meetings of the Council the Welsh language was clearly seen to be of crucial importance to our deliberations on primary education' (Gittins Report, p. 555). And he pointed out that the arguments used by the Council in support of their proposal that Welsh education should aim at a bilingual society were based on sentimentality and nationalism rather than on evidence (p. 556).

While there is no space here to analyse this long report, it is fair to conclude from it that for most of the members of the Council the desirability of preserving and reviving the language is an article of faith rather than a question for rational argument. Other reports, speeches and pamphlets give the same impression, and the 1972 manifesto of the Welsh Language Society confirmed that the impression is correct:

> The value of a literary and colloquial tradition is not a matter for objective analysis after weighing and measuring evidence. . . . To that astonishing question, 'Why do you want to keep up the Welsh language?' the true Welshman need only answer, 'That our fathers be not shamed.' (Translated version published in *Planet*, no. 26/27.)

Given this kind of fervour, it may be concluded that, whatever happens to the language, it is unlikely to fade away quietly. One well-informed Welsh journalist has said:

> The alternative to a full revival plan for Welsh is terrible to behold. It's not nice to see a man dying; it will be no nicer seeing the convulsions and death throes of a language. . . . Unless strong measures are taken before the arrival of the next census figures (presumably in 1983) I fear an escalation of protests which would not stop short of explosives. (Betts, pp. 213–14.)

It is of course difficult to judge whether frustrated language enthusiasts might use bombs to express their anger. But that the language issue is in a less literal sense explosive can hardly be doubted: for some Welshmen it is the most crucial issue of politics, and it is relevant to note the judgement of a leading Welsh political scientist that 'Welsh political culture is . . . shot through with Welsh cultural and national values and is thus inherently conducive to antagonism, anger and conflict' (Madgwick *(b)*).

The other complication is that Gwynfor Evans and his colleagues may be wrong in their assumption that the Welsh language is an essential basis of Welsh nationalism. The majority of Welshmen identify themselves as Welsh, whether or not they speak the language, and if they become convinced that a self-governing Wales would be better governed than it is in the United Kingdom they would presumably become nationalists. Some of the newer members of Plaid Cymru have social and economic objectives which they regard as more important than the language, and it was partly as a result of their influence that the long manifesto issued for the February 1974 election devoted 58 per cent of its content to social and economic issues. Plaid candidates actually got fewer votes in this election than they had in 1970, and this strengthens the arguments already given for doubting that the party is likely to change its character in the near future. But it is impossible to be sure about what will happen in the long run.

What Welsh nationalism lacks at the moment is an 'eruptive factor' which might transform it from a small and rather sectarian movement into one of mass appeal. If further economic difficulties and a growth of unemployment led to a crisis of confidence for the Labour Party in industrial Wales, and if this coincided with the discovery of an oilfield off the Welsh coast, conditions might favour the growth of a nationalist movement that was not based on the language issue. But whether developments will take this course can only be a matter for speculation.

8

English Nationalism and National Attitudes

> This royal throne of kings, this scepter'd isle,
> This earth of majesty, this seat of Mars,
> This other Eden, demi-paradise,
> This fortress built by Nature for herself
> Against infection and the hand of war,
> This happy breed of men, this little world,
> This precious stone set in the silver sea,
> Which serves it in the office of a wall,
> Or as a moat defensive to a house,
> Against the envy of less happier lands;
> This blessed plot, this earth, this realm, this England.
>
> Shakespeare, *Richard II*, Act II, Scene 1

The main political interest of these famous lines is that they are based upon a geographical error. Strictly speaking, England is not an island but only part of an island, comprising 55 per cent of its area. It is an error that has constantly been made over several centuries, even without the excuse of poetic licence. Disraeli often described himself as 'Prime Minister of England', Churchill called the English 'this island race', and the historian G. M. Trevelyan has written that when the English attempt to conquer France eventually failed in 1453 'England was left as a strange island anchored off the Continent' (Trevelyan, p. xii).

This common linguistic usage reflects the long-standing tendency of the English to make no clear distinction between 'England' and 'English' on the one hand and 'Britain' and 'British' on the other. Some of the reasons for this have been suggested in Chapter 3 and need not be recapitulated. But it is worth quoting an abbreviated extract from that final authority on the English language, Fowler's *Modern English Usage*.

England, English(man). The incorrect use of these words as equivalents of *Great Britain, United Kingdom, British Empire, British, Briton*, is often resented by the Scotch, Irish, and Welsh, their susceptibilities are natural, but are not necessarily always to be deferred to. It must be remembered that no Englishman, and perhaps no Scot even, calls himself a Briton without a sneaking sense of the ludicrous. How should an Englishman utter the words *Great Britain* with the glow of emotion that for him goes with *England*? He talks the *English* language; he has been taught *English* history . . . he has heard of the word of an *Englishman* and of *English* fair play, scorns certain things as *un-English*, and aspires to be an *English* gentleman; he knows that *England* expects every man to do his duty . . . in the word *England*, not in *Britain*, all these things are implicit. . . . The attempt to forbid thirty millions of people the use of the only names that for them are in tune with patriotic emotion, or to compel them to stop and think whether they mean their country in a narrower or a wider sense each time they name it, is doomed to failure. The most that can be expected is that the provocative words should be abstained from on the more provocative occasions, and that when Scots and others are likely to be within earshot *Britain* and *British* should be inserted as tokens, but no more, of what is really meant. (Fowler, p. 139.)

This guide was written in 1926 and reprinted frequently until the 1960s. In the second edition, revised by Sir Ernest Gowers and published in 1965, the entry is substantially the same except that the population has been increased to 'forty millions' and the last sentence has been tactfully omitted.

It follows that 'English nationalism' can be defined in two different ways:

(1) English nationalism can be defined as the determination of the English to maintain the independence, power and welfare of the British state they have created and dominated, in which case their objectives are shared by the majority of people in Scotland, Wales and Northern Ireland.
(2) English nationalism can be defined as the determination of the English to uphold and advance their own specific political interests in competition with the interests of the Scots, the Welsh and the Irish.

In practice English nationalism is invariably assumed to conform to the first of these definitions, both by those who regard the maintenance of the United Kingdom as desirable and beneficent and by those who look on the English as imperialists and describe the enlargement and political integration of the United Kingdom as a process of 'internal colonialism'. This view also conforms to the definition of 'possessive nationalism' put forward in Chapter 3, whereas the second definition would only qualify as a form of 'aspiring nationalism' if English spokesmen believed that the interests of England would be best served by the creation of a separate English state. The first definition will therefore be adopted as appropriate and English attitudes towards the other national groups within the United Kingdom will be discussed under the heading of 'English national attitudes'.

English/British Nationalism

The bases of national pride vary from one country to another. The English have never shared the French belief that their culture and civilisation are the best in the world, the German belief that they are in some sense a 'master-race', or the American belief that their democratic values and social relations are superior to all others. Nor have they taken any special pride in spiritual or religious matters, except in the negative sense that they are pleased to have broken away from the Roman Catholic Church. The main historical basis of English national pride lies rather in their military and naval prowess. One thing that every English schoolchild knows is that the English have never lost a war since 1066 – the little matter of the American colonies not counting as the colonists were themselves English.

By general consensus, the Tudor period was the greatest age of English history. This was not because of its system of government (which was somewhat tyrannical) but because in that age England defeated Spain, freed herself from the Vatican, and established herself as the world's foremost trading nation. Subsequent bases for national pride have been afforded by our victories over Napoleon, the establishment of the greatest empire and world has ever seen, and our two victories over Germany – particularly in the Second World War when for a time we stood alone against forces far superior to ours. Harold Macmillan has described the spirit of 1940 in a paragraph that illustrates the character of English nationalism rather well:

> Even the humblest could feel that they were taking part in the making of history. As the new Armada was being prepared against us, we seemed indeed the heirs of Queen Elizabeth and her captains. All the great figures of the past – Drake, Raleigh, Marlborough, Chatham, Wolfe, Pitt, Nelson, Wellington – seemed alive again and almost standing at our side. The

unity of the nation was complete and unshakeable. (Macmillan, p. xv.)

This selection of military and naval heroes as the great figures of English history is reflected in the monuments and names of buildings, streets and squares to be found in English cities. London has Waterloo Station and Waterloo Bridge, Trafalgar Square and Nelson's Column, but it does not have prominent buildings or thoroughfares named after politicians, poets or playwrights.

Since 1945, however, England has largely lost her traditional bases for national pride. Her defence has become entirely dependent on American support, and the two minor conflicts she has engaged in without that support – the Suez expedition and the Cod War with Iceland – both ended in humiliating withdrawals. The Empire has gone and the Commonwealth has become more of an embarrassment than an asset. On the economic front England has failed to adapt successfully to postwar conditions and since 1960 she has been overtaken, in terms of national income per head, by Germany, France, Holland, Belgium, Luxembourg, Denmark and Norway.

Since England's sources of national pride are now mainly a matter of history, there is a sense in which English nationalism falls outside all the categories listed in Chapter 3 and deserves a category of its own, best labelled 'nostalgic nationalism'. Certainly the most moving national ceremony is the annual Remembrance Day Service, when thousands gather to remember the dead of two world wars and join together in singing wartime songs. The Service attracts a television audience of about 11 million. It might be thought that English nationalism is confined to the middle-aged and elderly, but this is belied by the only other annual occasion which compares with the Remembrance Day Service, namely the last night of the Promenade Concerts (watched by about 8 million viewers). These symphony concerts have a youthful audience, many of whom stand in the vast auditorium, and on the last night they join with the orchestra in singing such songs as 'Rule, Britannia' and 'Land of Hope and Glory'. The latter is England's nearest approach to a national song and – given its words – the fervour with which it is sung by the Promenaders suggests that younger people share the nostalgic nationalism of their elders rather than that they have found a new source of national pride:

Land of Hope and Glory, Mother of the Free,
How shall we extol thee, who are born of thee?
Wider still and wider shall thy bounds be set;
God who made thee mighty, make thee mightier yet,
God who made thee mighty, make thee mightier yet.

Nostalgia for the past is not equivalent to pride in the present, and there is some evidence that feelings of national pride are relatively weak in contemporary England. A recent survey of English schoolchildren between the ages of 14 and 17 showed that only 48 per cent agreed with the proposition 'Britain is the best country in the world', compared with 76 per cent of American children who felt this about the United States (Dennis *et al.*, pp. 30–1). When asked whether the British system of government could be adopted by other countries with advantage, 51 per cent replied in the negative. When the equivalent question was put to American and German children, only 20 per cent of the Americans and 21 per cent of the Germans gave negative answers (pp. 32–3). The same survey showed that English children are more anarchistic in their attitudes than German, American or Italian children and are more sceptical about the performance of their government. Fifty-one per cent of English children thought that their government often, usually, or almost always makes mistakes compared with only 11 per cent of American children, 24 per cent of Italians, and 37 per cent of Germans (pp. 40–1).

It would be wrong to read too much into these figures, for another war of a conventional type would immediately rekindle the latent flames of English/British nationalism. But a conventional war is not imminent and the decline of English/British morale since 1945, and more rapidly since the economic crises of the 1960s, has undoubtedly reduced resistance to the appeals of the Scottish and Welsh nationalist movements.

English Attitudes towards Scotland, Ireland and Wales
As there are virtually no statistical data regarding these attitudes, generalisations about them have to be based on an interpretation of historical experience. In my understanding, English attitudes in the twentieth century can be characterised as tolerant, ill-informed and insensitive, and generally complacent.

To begin with the least flattering of these descriptions, there can be no doubt of the general ignorance among English people of the history and affairs of their Celtic neighbours. For generations the subject of history, as taught in schools and universities, has been divided into the main categories of 'English History' and 'European History', with the minor additions of colonial history and American history. But British history hardly exists. The English schoolchild is taught nothing about Scotland and Wales and learns about Ireland only as a problem to 'English' governments in the late nineteenth and early twentieth centuries. The inquiring adult finds that English libraries contain a superb literature on Irish history but a very thin literature on Scottish and Welsh history, so that, paradoxically, the educated classes are likely to know more about the history of what is now the Republic of Ireland than they do about the non-English parts of the United Kingdom. And, until as recently as the last decade, the available books on British government dealt almost entirely with English government.

This general ignorance leads to an unthinking kind of insensitivity. Until the debate on devolution got under way in 1975 the great majority of English people neither knew nor cared that Scotland had its own legal and educational systems, and were as likely to upset Scottish listeners by referring to 'the British educational system' as by talking about 'the English Parliament'. The English have also an enormous and constantly expanding repertoire of ethnic jokes, which many of their neighbours must regard as insensitive. Scottish people may not mind the stories which portray them as calculating, but can hardly enjoy those which portray them as mean. The constant flood of Irish jokes – currently between twenty and forty a week on television – are not likely to please Irish viewers. Some of them feature the twisted logic in which the Irish themselves take pleasure, as in (yesterday's example) the story of the Mother Superior who reacted to a nun's confession that she thought she was going to have a baby by saying 'Dear child, how can you be sure it's yours?' But too many of them revolve around the supposed inability of the Irish to count without using their fingers.

The Welsh rarely feature in these ethnic jokes, probably because Wales and England are now so closely integrated that the English tend to regard it as just another region. But the English language contains a verb that is by implication offensive, namely 'to welsh', defined in the *Concise Oxford Dictionary* as 'to decamp without paying'. The equivalent noun is 'welsher', universally used in England to describe a bookmaker who absconds before the winnings can be collected and frequently used in a more general sense to describe someone who defaults on his obligations. In 1975 the word became the subject of public controversy when a Cabinet minister accused miners who were demanding more pay of 'welshing on the social contract'. This drew an angry rebuke from one of his colleagues in the Cabinet, who represented a Welsh mining constituency, on the ground that the remark was not only unfair to miners but could also be regarded as an ethnic insult. It is unlikely that many Englishmen think about the ethnic connotation of the term when they use it, but it cannot fall happily on Welsh ears.

That the English are tolerant is also fairly clear. All studies of political culture have found toleration to be the most outstanding of the English political characteristics. To say that people are tolerant is not to say that they are so full of the milk of human kindness that (in P. G. Wodehouse's words) you can hear it sloshing about inside them when they walk down the street. Tolerance, properly defined, is a disposition to respect the right of political rivals and to give fair opportunities to members of groups recognised to be different. The English have never been accused of reserving political or administrative posts for themselves in either the British state or the British Empire. On the contrary, the opportunities have been open to all, and the Scots have probably taken more advantage of them, in proportion to their numbers, than the English have.

In Parliament, as we have seen, Scotland and Wales are overrepresented, as Ireland was also between 1855 and 1920. And the most outstanding example of English tolerance is the continued enfranchisement of Irish citizens in English elections, over fifty years after Ireland achieved independence and notwithstanding her neutrality in the Second World War and numerous unfriendly actions.

Some Welsh nationalists have accused the English of a lack of tolerance towards the Welsh culture, and history contains evidence of this from the sixteenth century to the end of the nineteenth century. But it takes a very special viewpoint to regard the contemporary English as ruthless and ambitious, willing to sacrifice the quality of life in Wales on the altar of material progress – which is a paraphrase of some remarks that have been made. Certainly there is no evidence that the average Welshman regards the English in this light, even in the rural areas. In 1971 a sample survey of public attitudes conducted in Cardiganshire, a rural county where three-quarters of the people spoke Welsh, included an open-ended question about their view of the English. The answers indicated that the most common opinion of the English was that they are pleasure-loving, happy-go-lucky and free with their money, less serious than the Welsh and apt to get more enjoyment from life (see Madgwick (a), pp. 86–7). This is not very different from the common Scottish view that the English are self-indulgent and permissive, and there is no evidence that a substantial body of opinion in either country regards the English as lacking in tolerance.

The last adjective suggested is 'complacent', in which connection it is perhaps worth quoting a well-known Scottish saying about the religious habits of their neighbours:

> The Irishman does not know what he believes but he'll
> fight to the death for it;
> The Welshman prays on his knees and his neighbours;
> The Englishman is a self-made man and he worships his creator.

The fact of English complacency is incontrovertible, though the economic problems of the past fifteen years have begun to dent it. What perhaps needs to be stressed in this context is the difficulty the English have in recognising the possibility of conflict until it actually breaks out, combined with the difficulty they have in understanding the deep attachment of most of the Irish and some of the Welsh to non-material values and symbols.

Not being very religious, most English people find it impossible to comprehend the intensity of the conflict in Northern Ireland. Not having long historical memories, they cannot understand why the Irish still commemorate battles and sieges of the seventeenth century. Not caring much about symbols, and taking their own national identity completely for granted, they are baffled by the Welsh nationalists' passionate concern for the Welsh language as a symbol of their nationhood. They can understand the Scottish nationalists much more easily, for their aims are mainly economic, but it was not until 1976 that the majority of English politicians – let alone the English public – woke up to the fact that the SNP poses a serious threat to the maintenance of the United Kingdom.

The bearing of these attitudes on government policies will be discussed in the next section. Before moving on to this, we must return to the question posed earlier, namely the extent to which the English have attitudes towards Scotland and Wales which are in any degree similar to the attitudes of Scottish and Welsh nationalists towards England. The conclusion must be that, as yet, they do not. They have shown very little concern to protect English interests, as distinct from the interests of Britain as a whole. They are internally divided on class lines, on ideological lines, and on regional lines, and these cleavages within England are far more important to English politicians and the English people than the divisions between England and her neighbours. As class and ideological cleavages reinforce one another, they dominate English politics, leaving English political leaders with little time or energy to devote to the affairs of what is sometimes called 'the Celtic fringe'.

It should also be noted that the English pay little attention to national symbols apart from those which relate to the United Kingdom. They do not celebrate St George's Day as the Scots and Welsh celebrate St Andrew's and St David's Day. They rarely fly the English flag and it is not certain that most Englishmen would even recognise it. They hardly ever sing national songs. During the Second World War they sang 'There'll Always Be an England' but in peacetime they would be deeply embarrassed by such a sentiment. When that super-patriotic boxer John H. Stracey defended his world championship in 1976, he entered the ring carrying a Union Jack and celebrated his victory by leading the audience in a rousing chorus of the only nationalistic song that could come easily to their lips, namely 'Maybe It's Because I'm a Londoner'.

The plans to establish Scottish and Welsh Assemblies have produced signs of what Scottish observers like to call 'an English backlash', but so far this has been singularly feeble. For instance, there has as yet been no demand for an English Assembly, which would be the most obvious way of defending English interests, except that made by the Liberal Party on the suggestion of its Scottish members.

English Attitudes and Government Policies

To understand the bearing of English attitudes on government policies towards Ireland and Wales in the twentieth century, it is necessary to take into account two other characteristics of modern English politicians. One of these is a deep reluctance to shed blood, a characteristic which was not nearly so pronounced during the nineteenth century and may be a reaction to the carnage of the First World War. The other is a strong preference for pragmatism and compromise, carried to the point at which it sometimes seems that English politicians are incapable of taking hard decisions when they are needed, preferring to wait until events have removed all the options but one. A comparison of the English (British) and French records in decolonisation highlights these characteristics rather well, for while the British have avoided any equivalent of the wars in Indo-China and Algeria they have also failed to equal the French success in establishing co-operative relationships with most of their former colonies and have remained encumbered with embarrassing relics of their former empire such as Rhodesia.

The attitude of London governments towards Irish affairs in the late nineteenth and twentieth centuries has shown a fairly consistent failure to understand the intensity of Irish conflicts together with a reluctance to intervene decisively until after the appropriate moment had passed. If the Land Act of 1903 had been introduced two or three decades earlier it might have forestalled the growth of Irish nationalism, for it dealt effectively with the main grievance that had troubled the Irish for generations. If the Liberal Government had introduced a proposal for Home Rule between 1906 and 1910, when it had a comfortable parliamentary majority without depending on the Irish Party, it would have had more authority and more room for maneouvre than it had in 1912. If Asquith and most of his colleagues had had a better understanding of Irish affairs they would not have been taken aback by the Ulster Protestant reaction to their proposals, and might have found a way of safeguarding the Protestants' interests without taking the country to the brink of civil war. Asquith's biography reveals a complacency about the Irish problem that is truly astonishing (see Spender and Asquith, chs 29–32).

The attitudes of London governments towards the problems of Northern Ireland have followed the same tradition. From 1922 until 1969 they took virtually no interest in the activities of the Stormont Government and did not think it their business to prevent the latter discriminating against Catholics, by measures such as gerrymandering with regard to local government elections. When British troops had to be flown to Northern Ireland in 1969 to keep the peace, the London government had a sudden attack of conscience. British troops could not be seen to be supporting an unfair regime, and the authorities in Belfast were quickly told to meet all the legitimate demands of the civil rights campaigners. But the expectation that this would pacify the campaigners was immediately proved fallacious, for the latter simply drew the lesson that militancy was the only way to secure political change. If London politicians had understood the Irish situation better they would not have been surprised by this, although it is of course arguable that the reforms were designed more to satisfy English public opinion than to remedy Catholic grievances.

When violence by the Irish Republicans increased the authorities responded by the introduction of internment and house-to-house searches for arms, just as in the nineteenth century they had responded to Irish lawlessness by intermittent campaigns of coercion. The consequences have already been described, and it must be added that the government was never willing to impose a curfew in Belfast and allow the security forces the latitude they needed if they were to get completely on top of the IRA. Coercion gave way to compromise and the power-sharing system was introduced at the insistence of Edward Heath and his colleagues. It did not last long, as knowledgeable students of Irish politics predicted, and it had two consequences that were unfortunate from the point of view of the Conservative Government in London. The first was that it destroyed the Ulster Unionist Party and ended the political career of its most agile and flexible leader, Brian Faulkner. The second, ironically, was that it led to the resignation of the Conservative Government after the general election of February 1974. At every election during the previous fifty years the Ulster Unionist MPs had been counted along with the Conservatives, and if this had been done in 1974 the Conservatives would have remained the largest single party. But as the Unionists were by then disgusted with Heath's policies in Ireland, they had to be counted as an independent group, with the result that Labour emerged as the largest single party and Heath had to advise the Queen to ask Harold Wilson to form a government.

The next crucial episode occurred in May 1974, when a group of Protestant trade unionists called a general strike in the Province with the intention of bringing the power-sharing executive to its knees. If the security forces had prevented the pickets from blocking the highways at the beginning of this strike it is unlikely that it would have gathered sufficient momentum to achieve this end. As it was, they sat on the sidelines for four days until the strike had become almost complete; were then called to hasty consultations in London as to how it could be broken; and finally concluded that this could not be done without employing methods that were thought to be politically unacceptable. In consequence the power-sharing experiment collapsed, and London is now saddled for an indefinite period with the responsibility of governing Northern Ireland directly, through a minister who acts in the manner of an old-fashioned colonial governor without the benefit of any elected local assembly to advise him or share in the responsibility for government decisions.

This is of course a very simplistic summary and it can be interpreted in various ways. From the point of view of the Irish Catholic community, it can be regarded as evidence of the ignorance and indifference of English politicians, reluctant to introduce reforms until events made these essential and offering 'too little and too late' to satisfy the Catholic community that their rights were properly appreciated. From the point of view of the Ulster Protestants, the record is evidence of the ignorance, unreliability and ingratitude of English politicians, who since 1969 have wantonly fulfilled the dearest wish of the Irish Republicans, namely to destroy the only Irish party capable of governing Northern Ireland. From the English point of view, the story is widely regarded as a not unsuccessful example of crisis management, in which two bloodthirsty private armies have been restrained from direct conflict and the death-rate has been kept reasonably low. Wherever one's sympathies lie, the crisis is a clear example of the contrast between the violent political culture of the Irish and the phlegmatic political culture of the English, in which the latter have tried to minimise the potential damage inherent in the situation without finding a policy that could reasonably be called a solution.

The political problems of contemporary Wales are of course infinitely less serious than those of Northern Ireland. In so far as Welsh problems differ from those of England, they revolve mainly around the position of the Welsh language. London governments have never devoted more than a minimum of time and attention to this issue but since the early sixties they have apparently felt some need to adopt an attitude towards it. This was not a political necessity because in the early sixties Plaid Cymru was not seen as an electoral threat. But the 1961 census figures made it clear that Welsh would virtually die out as a spoken language by the end of the century unless some action were taken, and impassioned protests by Welsh spokesmen pushed the authorities into some consideration of the matter.

If the issue is regarded in a rational and dispassionate manner, it would seem that there are two alternative policy positions that the government might have adopted with a reasonable hope of success. The first is to encourage the decline of the Welsh language. This will seem an outrageous statement to Welsh-speaking readers, but persuasive arguments can be adduced in its favour. Language differences divide one group from another in the most personal and socially disruptive ways. In his paper to the Fourteenth Nobel Symposium Arthur Koestler cited them as 'perhaps the main reason why the disruptive forces have always been stronger than the cohesive forces in our species' (Koestler, p. 22). Experience has amply demonstrated their tendency to produce political conflict and violence, most recently in Belgium, India, South Africa, Spain and Quebec.

In some countries the government has no choice but to cope with these conflicts, because the linguistic minorities are so substantial. But in Great Britain only 1 per cent of the population claims to speak Welsh and British governments do have a choice. They could, for instance, discourage the teaching of Welsh in schools, discourage radio and television authorities from broadcasting in Welsh, and forbid the use of the language in official business other than court proceedings (where it is clearly a fundamental right of citizens to give evidence in the language in which they feel best able to express themselves). Such a policy would go a long way towards eliminating the language problem within a generation and in cold logic there is a reasonable case for commending it.

The second logical alternative would be for the British government to decide that it is in the public interest that Welsh should be preserved as a living language and to take appropriate steps to further this objective. If policy-makers had studied the literature of sociolinguistics, they would have discovered that a minority language such as Welsh, which is not the normal language of business or the mass media, can be preserved only by one or other of two strategies. One of these is the cultivation of certain 'domains', meaning fields of activity, within which the language is the accepted medium of communication, and the other is the establishment of limited geographic areas within which the language is predominant (see, for instance, Fishman; Giglioli; and Pride and Holmes). It is now too late to pursue the first of these strategies, for the decline of religious observance has reduced the significance of the only public domain in which most people can participate where Welsh has remained the normal medium of communication.

However, it is not too late to pursue the second strategy, namely to delimit an area within which Welsh is still spoken by a majority of the inhabitants and to take positive steps to preserve the use of the language and enhance its status within this area. As noted in Chapter 5, this is the policy adopted in the Republic of Ireland, not because it was the first choice of Irish governments but because they have found it to be the only viable policy. And if this is the case in Ireland, it is even more certainly the case in Wales, which is far more closely integrated with England than Ireland has even been and far more industrialised, with only 5 per cent of its work-force engaged in agriculture compared with 31 per cent in the Republic.

This policy would not be endorsed by Welsh nationalists, because they see the language as a necessary basis for the Welsh

claim to be recognised as a nation; and it would not be endorsed
by the Welsh Language Society, whose aim is a rapid restoration
of the use of Welsh throughout the whole of Wales. But this
latter policy is absurdly unrealistic and has active support from
a very small minority. (The membership of the Society is only
about 3,000.) One sincere friend of the language has recommended a policy similar to that of the Irish Republic towards the
Gaeltacht, and has demonstrated that it would not be difficult
to define the area of the Welsh 'heartland', where over 70 per
cent of the people speak Welsh, though admittedly special provisions would be needed for five small towns within the area
which have become Anglicised and for a small 'transitional zone'
on the edges of the heartland (see Betts, chs 15 and 16). The
adoption of such a policy would be such an important step towards the preservation of the language that it should command
the support of all reasonable men who subscribe to that aim.

Faced with such a question, a French government might be
expected to adopt one or other of these logical alternatives.
Characteristically, British governments have adopted neither.
They are far too liberal and tolerant to adopt the first, but not
prepared to take enough interest in the problem to embark on
a serious discussion of the second. The pattern they have followed
since the early sixties can be roughly summarised as follows:
first, to provide opportunities for defenders of the language to
propose reforms; secondly, to accept most of these proposals in
principle and thus raise expectations; thirdly, to allow (or
encourage) officials and local authorities to drag their feet in the
implementation of the proposals, thus creating anomalies and
grievances; and, finally, to make various concessions, not in a
spirit of generosity or conviction but grudgingly and with bad
grace.

A significant move was made by the Conservative Government
in July 1963, when it appointed a committee under the chair-
manship of Sir David Hughes-Parry 'to clarify the legal status of
the Welsh language and to consider whether any changes in the
law ought to be made'. Two years later this committee recommended that laws and official business relating to Wales should
be based on the principle of 'equal validity', whereby Welsh
would have the same legal status as English. To this end, some
official forms should be printed in Welsh as well as in English,
wills written in Welsh should have full validity, a team of official
interpreters and translators should be established, courses in the
language should be organised for officials, proficiency in the
language should entitle civil servants to higher pay, and the head

of each government department in Wales should be a Welsh-speaker. The Labour Government that had come to power announced that they accepted this report with the exception of the two last recommendations, which were quite unacceptable to the civil service or the trade unions.

In practice, however, this declaration did not make as much difference to the situation as supporters of the language had hoped. In the absence of sanctions or incentive, the average civil servant did not rush to learn Welsh, a language which is not related to English or to any other language taught in English or Welsh schools. The Welsh Language Act which was introduced in 1967 was limited in scope. It clarified the right to use Welsh in legal proceedings, already largely established by the Welsh Courts Act of 1942, and it authorised government departments to print official forms in Welsh. But because the wording of many official forms is specified in Statutory Instruments – detailed pieces of supplementary legislation which are laid before Parliament by ministers – it transpired that these forms could not be printed in Welsh unless the minister concerned secured parliamentary authority for each translated form. There followed a series of agitations by supporters of the Welsh Language Society.

First there was an outcry because application forms for car licences were not available in Welsh, and some motorists refused to apply on an English form. When it became clear that demonstrators were willing to face court actions over this issue, the matter was discussed in the Cabinet. It was agreed that Welsh application forms would be printed, but that they would have to be sent in by post to a government office rather than dealt with over the counter at a Post Office, as most Post Office clerks could not read Welsh. This decision provoked further demonstrations in Post Offices, in response to which the authorities gave way again.

It had been specifically decided that the licence issued, in the form of a disc which is displayed on the windscreen, should not be printed in Welsh, a logical decision in its way since the information on the disc is for the benefit of the police. The government indeed announced firmly that it did not propose to issue a Welsh or bilingual car licence disc either then (in 1969) or at any time in the future. To challenge this, 200 professional people, including professors, ministers of religion, doctors, librarians, and newspaper editors, signed a declaration that they would not display a disc printed in English and that if they were fined for this offence (as many younger people had been already) they would go to prison rather than pay (see R. Lewis, p. xix).

When faced with this challenge the government grudgingly climbed down and started to print discs in both languages.

This ham-handed approach to the issue of government forms, of which the car licence controversy is only one example, was paralleled by the attitude of the Welsh Office to traffic signs. These signs were not covered by the Welsh Language Act but in November 1967 the Welsh Secretary said in answer to a Parliamentary Question that he was prepared to authorise local authorities to erect bilingual signs if this was requested. The reply was widely publicised in Wales, but when the Lleyn Rural District Council requested permission to erect such signs it was told that it had to make an individual application for each sign-post (see R. Lewis, pp. 88–90, for the correspondence). This raising and dashing of expectations led to a campaign of direct action by the Welsh Language Society, whose members painted over monolingual traffic signs, were arrested and fined, and in some cases went to prison for refusing to pay the fines. The eventual result of this campaign was that bilingual road signs have been erected all over Wales, serving no real purpose save to advertise the language and stand as symbols of Welsh identity. In this way the British authorities have played straight into the hands of the Welsh nationalist movement.

Yet another example relates to the demand for television pro-grammes in Welsh. After a good deal of discussion between the various authorities and groups concerned, it has been agreed in principle that if a fourth channel is created in Wales it will be devoted to Welsh broadcasts. This is a very odd proposition since Welsh-speakers form only 1 per cent of the British population and if a Welsh channel were to have only 1 per cent of the BBC licence fees this would be totally inadequate, with no reservoir of films or videotapes to draw on. It would make much more sense to establish a radio programme in the language, which is what the Irish Republic has now done for the Gaeltacht. As it is, a vague promise of television has been made which is unlikely to be fulfilled.

This manner of governing reflects the mixture of tolerance and indifference with which English politicians and administrators regard the language issue. It has provoked a minority of language enthusiasts into forms of direct action which have repeatedly induced government departments to eat their words and thus, to a limited extent, eroded the authority of the democratic process. It has provided gratuitous propaganda for the Welsh nationalist movement. And worst of all for the people of Wales, the confused situation regarding the language has led to the development of linguistic conflict. Welsh language enthusiasts have developed the habit of speaking in Welsh to telephone operators and other public officials, many of whom can only speak English; of accusing non-Welsh-speaking Welshmen of being in some sense traitors to their own nation; and of refusing to speak English to the children of English migrants (which is the stated policy of the Welsh Language Society). This kind of behaviour naturally causes resentment and even bitterness, and the Archbishop of Wales is only one of several distinguished Welshmen who have warned of its dangers. In 1968 he said:

> There is a real danger of a Belgian situation here, or even a kind of apartheid based not on race but on language. . . . It is intolerable that those who do not speak Welsh should be regarded as second-class citizens, or less genuine lovers of their country than their bilingual compatriots. (Quoted in Philip, p. 334.)

English politicians and administrators would undoubtedly say that it is not their fault if Welshmen behave unpleasantly towards one another over the language issue, just as it is not their fault if Irishmen shoot one another over the religious issue. Up to a point this is a reasonable argument, particularly since any firm English initiative on the matter would cause resentment in Wales. The instinct of English politicians in this kind of situation is to create a local institution to deal with the matter, whether it be an advisory council or a Welsh Assembly. It might be said that the reports of Welsh advisory committees in recent years have been unhelpful with regard to the language issue and that the creation of a Welsh Assembly at this juncture would exacerbate conflicts over the language which are potentially explosive. But if London governments lack the resolution to impose an effective policy, it is certainly arguable that they ought to hand the issue over to Welsh politicians and let them cope with it themselves.

The problems posed by Scottish nationalism are much more easily comprehended by English politicians, who are consequently more prepared to cope with them. The character of the English response to Scottish nationalism will be discussed in the following chapter.

9

The Devolution Proposals

It is evident that the growth of Scottish nationalism poses a much more serious and urgent threat to the continued existence of an integrated British state than the growth of Welsh nationalism does. The SNP increased its share of the Scottish vote from 11 per cent in the 1970 election to 22 per cent in February 1974 and 30 per cent in October 1974. With four parties in competition it would require only a relatively small increase in SNP support to give the nationalists a clear majority of Scottish seats at the next election: in October 1974 Labour won 41 of the 71 seats with 36 per cent of the total vote.

Since public opinion polls show that about 80 per cent of Scottish voters and well over 90 per cent of all British voters are opposed to the separation of Scotland from the United Kingdom, it is the clear duty of the British Government to take steps to avert the constitutional crisis that would undoubtedly ensue if the SNP were to win a majority of Scottish seats. The instrument fashioned by the government for this purpose is the Scotland and Wales Bill, introduced in November 1976 and currently under discussion in Parliament. As this Bill will be passed, amended or defeated by the time this book is published it would be inappropriate to enter into a detailed analysis of the Bill's provisions. It will, however, be illuminating to discuss its antecedents, the logic of its basic proposals and the possible consequences of such institutional changes as may be adopted.

In a sense, the first shot in what has become the devolution debate was fired in November 1967, when Winifred Ewing won a by-election for the SNP in the previously safe Labour seat of Hamilton. Within eighteen months the government had appointed a Royal Commission on the Constitution, 'to examine the present functions of the central legislature and government in relation to the several countries, nations and regions of the United Kingdom' and to consider 'whether any changes are desirable'.

To some extent, the Scottish Conservative and Unionist Association had anticipated this development by establishing its own committee under Sir William McEwan Younger to investigate the need for Scottish devolution. Following this, Edward Heath declared at the 1968 annual conference of the Scottish Association that he favoured the creation of a Scottish Assembly and was asking Sir Alec Douglas-Home to chair another committee to make detailed proposals about the reform. This committee reported in 1970 and recommended the establishment of a directly elected Assembly which would act rather in the manner of a third House of Parliament, having power to question Scottish ministers, discuss government policy, and take the Second Reading and Committee stages of all Scottish legislation. There were obvious problems about this proposal, notably the possibility of conflict between a Conservative Government in London and a Scottish Assembly with a non-Conservative majority in Edinburgh, and the Conservative Government of 1970–4 made no attempt to introduce the change. The genesis of the present Bill is to be found rather in the deliberations of the Royal Commission and the tactical plans of the Labour Party.

The Royal Commission considered a mass of written and verbal evidence, secured expert advice in a number of research reports, and sponsored a large-scale survey of public attitudes to political and constitutional questions. The members of the Commission came round to the unanimous view that changes in the machinery of government were desirable, but when their report was published in October 1973 its political impact was relatively slight. One reason for this was that at the time of its publication attention was focused on the Arab–Israeli conflict and the oil embargo. Another reason was that, while the commissioners agreed on their objective, they disagreed on the methods of securing it, producing a main report in which four different schemes of devolution were proposed and a long Memorandum of Dissent proposing a fifth.

As Brian Chapman has pointed out, the British tradition with regard to royal commissions is by European standards rather odd (Chapman, p. 32). Although an enormous amount of effort goes into their inquiries, neither Parliament nor the government of the day feels under an obligation to accept their recommendations. As it was known in the autumn of 1973 that English Conservative MPs were sceptical about the proposal for a Scottish Assembly made by their Scottish colleagues and hostile to the idea of a Welsh Assembly, it seemed unlikely that the Conservative Government would be in any hurry to adopt the Royal Commission's proposal to create such assemblies. And as representatives of the Labour Party in Scotland had expressed uncompromising hostility to the idea of a Scottish Assembly, while the General Council of the Trades Union Congress had indicated its dislike of any delegation or division of legislative powers, some observers thought that the Report had little chance of being implemented (for Labour Party views, see *Minutes of Evidence*, vol. IV, pp. 23–33; for TUC views, see *Written Evidence*, vol. 9, pp. 95–6).

The whole scene changed as a consequence of the sensational gains by the SNP in the general election of February 1974. The Labour Party quickly commissioned a survey of marginal seats, the results of which were leaked to Scottish newspapers in May 1974 and indicated that thirteen Labour seats were in danger of falling to the SNP. The National Executive Committee of the Labour Party (henceforth NEC) set up a Working Group on Devolution in the same month. This was the main item on the agenda of party meetings held in both Scotland and Wales on 22 June 1974, but whereas the Labour Party in Wales called for an elected Welsh Assembly the Executive Committee of the Scottish Council of Labour rejected the idea of a Scottish Assembly by six votes to five. Four days later the NEC in London asked the Scottish Committee to convene a special one-day conference to discuss the issue, and this was held on 17 August. By this time the NEC had approved a motion by Alex Kitson, a leading Scottish trade unionist, calling for the creation of a Scottish Assembly with legislative powers, and trade union votes swung the Scottish conference behind this policy. In September the NEC published a policy statement proposing elected assemblies for both Scotland and Wales and two weeks later the Labour Government published a White Paper containing the same proposal.

This sequence of events makes clear that the effective reason for the Government's commitment to devolution was the electoral threat to the Labour Party rather than the Royal Commission's report (henceforth referred to as the Kilbrandon Report). However, the Report contained arguments and proposals that had an influence on subsequent policy and their logic deserves some attention.

The Kilbrandon Report

In point of fact, many of the Report's basic arguments were somewhat outdated by 1974. The main reason for the rapid growth of the SNP was disenchantment with the economic and industrial relations policies of successive London governments, combined with the discovery of a major oilfield in the North Sea. But many of the arguments for reform in the Kilbrandon Report were based on the Attitudes Survey that had been conducted in the summer of 1970 on the basis of a brief prepared during the previous winter.

The climate of opinion in the winter of 1969–70 was very different from the climate in 1974: after several years of economic crisis and wage restraint in the mid-sixties, the balance of payments was (temporarily) favourable, and government spokesmen were declaring rather frequently that they had 'got the economy right'. The fashionable complaint in 1969 was that the British system offered inadequate opportunities for 'participation' (the word in vogue) in the political process, and this was the main problem which the Royal Commission set out to investigate. It was claimed that the investigations of the Commission revealed fairly widespread dissatisfaction with the British democratic system, particularly with the centralisation of power in London, and this was the main reason given in the Kilbrandon Report for the reforms that were proposed (see Kilbrandon Report, pp. 329–31).

The evidence for these arguments in the Attitudes Survey is actually very slender. The Survey revealed that, of the 4,892 persons interviewed, 62 per cent were satisfied with the way things are run in Britain and that there was more dissatisfaction with local authorities than with the national government (Commission on the Constitution, Research Paper 7, p. 21). Only 10 per cent of the respondents had ever felt like complaining to the civil service, compared with 26 per cent who had felt like complaining to their local council office, 25 per cent to each of British Rail and the local gas board, 19 per cent to the local electricity board, 18 per cent to large private firms, and 16 per cent to the National Health Service (p. 29). Only 3 per cent had taken a grievance to their MP compared with 18 per cent who had complained to their local council office, and 63 per cent of the former were satisfied with the way their complaint had been dealt with compared with only 45 per cent of the latter (pp. 25–6).

When people were asked to say what they would like to see done to improve things in their region, only 3 per cent spontaneously said that they would like more say for people in the area as against central government, compared with 21 per cent who wanted better roads, 20 per cent who wanted better leisure facilities and 20 per cent who wanted more economic development. Of the fourteen types of improvement mentioned, more local democracy was in fact the least popular. The answers in Scotland and Wales differed from those in England, with 20 per cent of Scottish respondents and 9 per cent of the Welsh advocating more local democracy. But even in these countries the desire for decentralisation was overshadowed by other desires: thus, 47 per cent of the Scots and 51 per cent of the Welsh wanted more economic development.

It was only when decentralisation was suggested to respondents that the majority of them indicated that they approved of it. In one question respondents were asked whether or not they agreed with the proposition: 'If this region had more say in running its own affairs, things would be run more efficiently in the region.' This was a question which clearly invited an affirmative answer and generally got one. In the ten regions of England 79 per cent of respondents agreed and only 13 per cent disagreed. In Scotland (described as a region in the Survey) 76 per cent agreed and 19 per cent disagreed. In Wales 62 per cent agreed and 30 per cent disagreed (p. 75).

This Welsh response is superficially at odds with the fact that the Welsh were more apt than the English to suggest decentralisation spontaneously. But the answers are fully compatible with what we know of Welsh nationalism, which is fervently supported by a minority but actively disliked by many others. This sharp split in Welsh opinion, though never discussed in the Kilbrandon Report, showed up again in the responses given when people were asked to choose between various policies regarding devolution, as can be seen in Table 9.1.

Table 9.1   *Preferred Devolution Policy in 1970*

Preferred Policy	England (mean of 10 regions) %	Scotland %	Wales %
Leave things as they are	38	25	42
Some devolution of decision-making to region	23	26	21
Extensive or complete devolution to region	37	47	36

Source: Commission on the Constitution, Research Paper 7, Table 45.

If this evidence is viewed impartially it suggests that there was a fairly strong public demand for devolution in Scotland but that opinion in Wales was divided and marginally less favourable to devolution than opinion in England. Some of the other responses suggest that people were motivated more by the hope of economic advantage than by the ambition to increase democratic participation in politics. While 61 per cent of the whole sample indicated (when it was suggested to them) that they would like at least a moderate degree of devolution of decision-making, only 30 per cent agreed that they would still like this if it meant that people in other regions were better off financially than people in their region, and only 10 per cent would still favour devolution if it meant that people in their region would be worse off than under the existing system. There is nothing surprising about these figures but it is surprising that the Royal Commission adhered throughout its four and a half years to its original position that the essential problem was the quality of democracy rather than the performance and benefits of the system.

Whether because or in spite of the evidence of public attitudes revealed by the Survey, eight of the thirteen members of the Commission favoured the creation of legislative assemblies for Scotland and Wales. As Northern Ireland already had such an assembly the logical concomitant of this proposal would clearly be the creation of an assembly for England, or several assemblies for the regions of England, thus giving the United Kingdom a federal or quasi-federal form of government. This solution has long been advocated by the only British party which has favoured devolution without disintegration, namely the Liberal Party, and it is surprising that it was rejected outright by the Commission.

The Kilbrandon Report gave four reasons for rejecting a federal solution, all of which are open to question. First, it was said that federalism is an inconvenient system of government. Most democrats would include the federal systems of the United States, Canada, Australia, Switzerland and West Germany in a short list of the world's most successful systems of government, but the Commissioners took the view that if these systems had worked well it was because those concerned with government had been successful in overcoming their drawbacks. And it was said that in both Canada and the United States 'the constitutional division of sovereignty between the federal and provincial governments has made it difficult to achieve the kind of system the people really need' (Kilbrandon Report, p. 157).

Secondly, it was said that the English people would not want such a system. The Report declared roundly that 'the English people would generally regard it as inappropriate to have a separate legislature for England; and there is no public demand for English regional assemblies with legislative powers, whether under a federal system or otherwise' (p. 353). This is a very peculiar statement, for the evidence quoted above shows that 37 per cent of the English people interviewed said that they would like a reform giving extensive or complete devolution of decision-making powers to regional authorities. If assemblies were created for Scotland and Wales the English would be fools if they did not demand the same political rights as their neighbours. The question of how many English assemblies would be appropriate is one to which various answers can be given, but the German experience suggests that this need not be a major stumbling-block. Some of the *lander* created in 1946 had rather artificial boundaries, but they have nevertheless attracted the loyalty of their citizens as a consequence of their activities (see Commission on the Constitution, Research Paper 1, p. 56).

Thirdly, it was said that a federation of four states would be unrealistic and unworkable because England, with 83 per cent of the population, would dominate the whole system. In the highly unlikely circumstance that the English parties combined together against the other states this would of course be true, but in this circumstance the English dominance would be much less complete under a federal system than under a unitary system, for large areas of policy in Scotland, Wales and Northern Ireland would be controlled by their own legislative assemblies. This argument must therefore be regarded as exaggerated.

The final argument put forward against a federal solution was that even if England were divided into provinces the system would be unbalanced, since 'the province which included south-east England might well itself dominate the federation' (p. 159). It is difficult to consider this argument without impatience. The proportion of the population living in the south-east (31 per cent) is smaller than the proportion of Canadians living in Ontario, and it is not generally thought that Ontario dominates Canada in such a way as to make Canadian federalism unworkable. As pointed out in Chapter 3, official policies since 1945 have shown a bias against the south-east and the midlands which goes beyond what can be justified in economic terms and must be ascribed partly to provincial jealousy and party-political discrimination.

The membership of the Royal Commission itself was geographically biased. It so happens that almost exactly half (49 per cent) of the UK population live in the south-eastern quadrant of the country (the two midlands regions plus the south-eastern region and East Anglia), but only three of the eleven Commissioners who signed the main Report came from this quadrant, the others comprising two members from Scotland, two from Wales, one from Northern Ireland, two from the north of England, and one from the far south-west. But even so, it is surprising to find them expressing such apparent hostility to the south-east.

The several recommendations of the Royal Commission must now be outlined briefly. Six members favoured the establishment of legislative assemblies in both Scotland and Wales with a wide range of powers, which would however not include economic planning and related issues. There would be Scottish and Welsh governments responsible to these assemblies. The revenue put at the disposal of the Scottish and Welsh governments would be decided annually by an Exchequer Board which would receive estimates from the UK government as well as from those of Scotland and Wales and decide on an allocation which would enable all areas of the United Kingdom to have public services of equivalent standard. If the allocation included the revenue of devolved taxes it would be open to the Scottish and Welsh governments to levy those taxes at rates which were either higher or lower than the nominal rate assumed for the purpose of calculating the allocation within a margin to be agreed. The Scottish and Welsh governments could distribute their expenditure as they chose, providing higher standards than the national average in some services, offset by lower standards in others.

It was not proposed by this group that there should be any assemblies for England, and it was recognised that this would be unfair. It was proposed that the representation of Scotland and Wales in Parliament should be the same as that of England, in proportion to their respective populations, and their remarks on the justice of this arrangement are worth quoting in full:

> No scheme of representation at Westminster can be devised which would satisfactorily reflect the fact that Parliament would be legislating for England on matters for which in Scotland and Wales it had transferred legislative responsibility to Scottish and Welsh Assemblies. Even if the representation of Scotland and Wales were reduced to parity with England, a serious injustice would be done to the people of England.
>
> The supporters of legislative devolution do not consider that the English people would in fact have any feeling of injustice, or that the admitted difficulty about representation should be allowed to stand in the way of a desirable measure of devolution. (p. 344.)

This view, put forward by two Scotsmen, two Welshmen, one Ulsterman and one Englishman, seems therefore to rest on the assumption that the English people are so apathetic or tolerant or complacent that they would not mind being governed under a constitution that patently discriminated against them.

The other English members were divided in their recommendations. Two advocated a legislative assembly for Scotland but thought that Wales should have an assembly with only deliberative and advisory functions. One (the only identifiably Conservative member) advocated councils with deliberative and advisory functions for both Scotland and Wales, with the addition in the case of the Scottish Council of some powers in relation to parliamentary legislation. It was thought that the Council could take the Second Reading and Committee stages of Scottish Bills, as suggested by the Douglas-Home Committee, and might also take the Third Reading if the Leader of the House of Commons agreed. Two members, who believed in the principle of uniformity, recommended a scheme of executive devolution to regional councils in each of the eight English regions (as defined for purposes of economic planning), as well as to councils in Scotland and in Wales.

The Memorandum of Dissent

Two members of the Commission felt unable to sign the main Report and their recommendations were published in a Memorandum of Dissent. These were in fact the only two social scientists on the Commission, Lord Crowther-Hunt of Oxford University and Professor Alan Peacock of York University. Their Memorandum is a much more coherent and persuasive document than the main Report.

One reason for this is that the authors did not have Lord Kilbrandon's problem of having to maximise agreement among a group of people who manifestly had differing ideas, a problem that may have been compounded by the fact that Lord Kilbrandon did not become Chairman until the Commission had been at work for almost three years, following the death of the former Chairman.

Another reason is that the authors were not confined to the normal procedure of British royal commissions, which is somewhat peculiar. Their main method of work is to cross-examine witnesses who volunteer to present views on the subject at issue. The commissions cannot subpoena witnesses and those who volunteer normally have special axes to grind. This may not matter too much when the subject is a specialised one involving particular interest groups who can all be expected to defend themselves, but it does matter when the subject affects the lives of ordinary citizens who may not have spokesmen for their views. In this case, as Crowther-Hunt and Peacock point out, the great majority of those who gave evidence 'about the state of affairs in Wales were middle-class Welsh-speaking Welshmen', and thus unrepresentative of the majority of Welsh citizens (see *Memorandum of Dissent*, p. 10).

Moreover, royal commissions do not normally supplement the evidence offered by making their own investigations, and indeed cannot do so as their members (who are unpaid) are busy men who have little time to spare. As academics, Crowther-Hunt and Peacock may have had more time at their disposal, and as social scientists they were familiar with the very extensive literature that is relevant to the issues under discussion. In consequence, the Memorandum not only contains a clearer analysis of the Attitudes Survey than was made in the main Report but also draws on a good deal of other relevant evidence.

The Memorandum made out a persuasive case for giving the people of England the same kind of devolution as that given to the Scots and the Welsh. It was pointed out that the people of Scotland were only marginally more in favour of devolution than the people in most English regions – the figures being 73 per cent in Scotland compared with 69 per cent in the North West of England, 66 per cent in the South, 65 per cent in the East Midlands and 62 per cent in Yorkshire. As this question rather invited an affirmative answer, the authors also compared the proportions who said they were in favour of the most extreme form of devolution considered (i.e. that the region should 'take over complete responsibility for running things' in the area). The proportions were 23 per cent in Scotland compared with 21 per cent in the South, 20 per cent in East Anglia, between 18 and 16 per cent in most other English regions, and only 13 per cent in Wales (*Memorandum of Dissent*, pp. 26–7). It is argued that in view of these figures there are no firm grounds for giving devolution to Scotland and Wales while denying it to the English regions.

The Memorandum took a much broader view of the problems involved than the main Report had done, for the majority of the members of the Royal Commission had adopted a narrow interpretation of their terms of reference, leading them 'to concentrate on . . . the case for devolution as far as Scotland and Wales are concerned, and to commend it in an extreme form; whereas the case for devolution should have been considered as one (among many other) possible alternative or complementary changes in our system of government as a whole' (p. 52). The authors of the Memorandum set out a number of principles which formed the basis of their proposals and can be briefly summarised as follows:

(1) that citizens in all parts of the United Kingdom should have the same political rights and obligations;
(2) that citizens, through their elected representatives, should be given more control over decision-making processes in government than they now enjoy;
(3) that to preserve the unity of the United Kingdom, and to avoid complications in regard to the EEC, there should be no devolution of legislative powers from Parliament to subordinate assemblies.

The application of these principles led the authors of the Memorandum to propose the creation of seven new elected assemblies, one for Scotland, one for Wales, and one for each of five English regions. These assemblies would have power to allocate funds between differing public services in their area and to supervise the work of local authorities. They would also take over control of the regional offices of central government departments, and the functions of the numerous *ad hoc* public authorities operating in their areas, such as regional health authorities and water authorities. In the case of commercial and industrial authorities, such as the gas and electricity boards, the new assemblies would not have control but would have the power to make byelaws and ordinances to give effect to their decisions and – most important – they would have powers to raise revenue, by means such as retail sales taxes and a supplementary income tax.

This scheme would give the Scottish Assembly control over the Scottish Office, and would thus meet the complaints that have been made about the shortage of parliamentary time for questions to the Secretary of State for Scotland. It would also give the English regions the power that they do not now enjoy to draw up plans for the development of their region and to impose their own priorities on public expenditure. It would increase the democratic element in the British system of government without (it was claimed) adding appreciably to the size and cost of the administration; for the officials who would come under the control of the assemblies are already working in the regions, either for departments of the central government or for *ad hoc* authorities. It would, of course, increase the number of elected representatives, but as the local government reforms of 1972–4 reduced the number of elected representatives in Great Britain by 14,500 the authors of the Memorandum felt it would be reasonable to assume that candidates would be forthcoming for the 700 seats they proposed for the assemblies.

The Memorandum also suggested changes in parliamentary procedure involving greater use of functional committees. They endorsed the 1967 proposal of the House of Commons Select Committee on Procedure that 'the House should be brought in at an earlier point in the legislative process so as to allow discussion by Parliament of subjects and details of potential legislation before the Government finally prepare a Bill'. And they suggested that MPs would have more time to work in this way if they were relieved of much of their work dealing with the grievances of constituents against local bureaucrats, which would be taken over by members of the new assemblies (pp. 113–15).

The Memorandum also suggested that the House of Lords should be strengthened by 150 new members, comprising 25 from each of the Scottish and Welsh assemblies and 20 from each of the five English regional assemblies. It was suggested that a House of Lords enlarged in this way could reasonably be given an additional function, namely to scrutinise all legislation and statutory instruments to ensure that they did not restrict the powers and discretion of the new regional authorities.

The Memorandum contained many detailed arguments and proposals which cannot be summarised here. But enough has been said to indicate that the Memorandum presented a coherent and well-argued scheme of reform that would treat all citizens of the kingdom equally. When Lord Crowther-Hunt was appointed in 1974 as an adviser to the Labour Government on constitutional questions, some observers thought that this might mean that the Government would accept the general approach to the problem set out in the Memorandum of Dissent. But these observers misunderstood the tactical plans being made by Labour Party leaders.

Labour Party Tactics
When Labour leaders considered their tactics in 1974–5, they had before them the five alternative plans for devolution that had been suggested by members of the Royal Commission. In order to understand the tactics adopted, it is necessary to appreciate two points. The first is that most Labour leaders do not believe in devolution for its own sake, but only as a device to preserve their electoral position against competition from nationalist parties. This is in no way surprising. Since 1945 Labour has been the most centralising of the British parties, more apt than the others to reduce the powers of local government in the cause of promoting uniform standards. Its economic and fiscal policies have been equalitarian in a geographical as well as a personal

sense, and the Scottish Labour spokesman who gave evidence to the Royal Commission argued with some force that the best thing for Scotland is to have a Labour government in London giving Scotland special assistance out of public funds.

However, to combat the challenge of the SNP, Labour leaders have thought it necessary to introduce a Bill proposing a Scottish Assembly with a wide range of legislative powers. As the situation in Wales is different in various ways, one of which is that the electoral challenge from the nationalists is less serious, it is proposed that Wales should have an assembly with executive powers but no legislative powers. And as there is no electoral threat from English nationalists, it is not proposed that any change be made in England.

The proposal for a Scottish Assembly follows the precedent established by the creation of the Northern Ireland Parliament half a century ago. When this was done the representation of Northern Ireland at Westminster was cut to two-thirds of what it should have been in terms of population in consideration of the fact that Irish citizens also had their own Parliament. If this precedent were followed for Scotland, the number of Scottish representatives at Westminster would be reduced to two-thirds of 57, namely 38.

However, the second basic fact underlying the Government's proposals is that Labour normally does much better in Scotland than the Conservative Party. In the eight general elections since the 1948 Representation of the People Act, Labour has won a majority of Scottish seats six times and tied with the Conservatives on one occasion, whereas in England Labour has won a majority of seats only once and got a plurality on another occasion. In Wales Labour has won a majority of seats in all eight elections, so that three of the five overall electoral victories for Labour in this period have depended on the party's advantage in Scotland and Wales. In view of this it is proposed that the Scottish representation at Westminster should not be reduced at all, not even to the parity figure of 57 which the Kilbrandon Report had the grace to recommend.

This can only be described as a crude gerrymander. It has the immediate effect of making Conservative opposition to the Bill inevitable, thus denying any possibility that a profoundly important constitutional change might be carried through with some measure of all-party agreement. If the proposal is enacted, it will have two further consequences. One is that the over-large contingent of Scottish MPs will be in a very curious position, having power over a whole range of contentious issues affecting the

English people without having any power to influence policies in these areas in Scotland.

The second consequence would be to increase the likelihood of a constitutional crisis leading to disintegration. As the proposed contingent of 71 Scottish MPs is almost twice as large as it would be if the Northern Ireland precedent were followed, the proposal almost doubles the statistical chances of the SNP holding the balance of power in a future Westminster Parliament. It was suggested in an earlier chapter that English political conflicts invariably loom larger in the eyes of English politicians than the problems of their Celtic neighbours, and it would seem that the present leaders of the Labour Party are more concerned to safeguard their electoral position in relation to the Conservatives than they are to safeguard the United Kingdom against the threat of political disintegration.

While this central feature of the Scotland and Wales Bill favours Scotland unduly, other features of the Bill so limit the legislative powers of the proposed Scottish Assembly that it seems unlikely to satisfy the demands of voters who have transferred, or are thinking of transferring, their allegiance to the SNP because of the manifest failure of London governments in the field of economic management. Such voters will be disappointed to find that the Bill gives the Assembly no legislative powers in relation to economic planning and development, and (of course) no powers over North Sea oil.

Within the legislative fields which are devolved, Scottish legislation will still be subject to a veto by the Westminster Parliament (which in practice means by the UK government) if 'an Assembly Bill is considered by the Government to have unacceptable repercussions on matters for which they remain responsible' (*Devolution to Scotland and Wales: Supplementary Statement*, p. 3). Not surprisingly, this provision was attacked by SNP spokesmen as 'an insult to Scotland', and it is noteworthy that the day after the Bill was presented *The Scotsman* (not a nationalist paper) carried the banner headline: 'Veto casts long shadow over Scots Assembly' (*The Scotsman*, 1 December 1976).

Yet another limitation of the Bill is that it makes no provision for either the Scottish or the Welsh Assembly to levy taxation. The Kilbrandon Report had suggested that petrol duty, vehicle excise duty, retail sales taxes and a supplementary income tax were all possible sources of revenue for a Scottish or Welsh authority. But the Government has rejected these suggestions on the dubious ground that they would be administratively complex. The absence of any power to raise revenue would not only be a serious handicap to the Scottish and Welsh authorities (which in this respect would have less power than a district council) but would also enable Scottish and Welsh politicians to blame the meanness of London governments for the shortcomings of their public services. By this decision the authors of the Bill have deprived future United Kingdom governments of one of the main political advantages that might be derived from the creation of Scottish and Welsh assemblies, namely to divert criticisms and discontent from London to Edinburgh and Cardiff.

The Scottish and Welsh authorities will get their revenue in the form of an annual block grant. The experience of federal countries has shown how much conflict between the regional and central governments can arise from the determination of grants, and also that the most satisfactory way of minimising the conflict is to hand the issue over to a semi-autonomous commission such as the Australian Commonwealth Grants Commission. The Kilbrandon Report suggested that an Exchequer Board should be created to fulfil this function.

However, the Goverment has taken the view that the determination of the block grants is a political issue which has to be settled by bargaining and resolved by a decision of the UK government. The result would be an annual auction supplemented by further auctions whenever the government was forced to impose public expenditure cuts between one annual budget and another. It is difficult to resist the suspicion that this arrangement has been favoured because Labour leaders think their party would be able to outbid the Conservatives in financial generosity towards Scotland and Wales. This suspicion has already occurred to politicians in the industrial north-east of England, where the Labour-dominated Tyne and Wear County Council has passed a resolution condemning the Government's proposals on the ground that they would 'bring about an economic imbalance favourable to Scotland at the expense of the north-eastern region' (*The Scotsman*, 6 January, 1976).

Conclusion

With these crippling defects, the Scotland and Wales Bill cannot be regarded as a sensible attempt to prevent the disintegration of the United Kingdom while satisfying the wish of many Scottish and Welsh voters for more control over their own affairs. It proposes a system of government which would be unlikely to stabilise the situation and is not wanted for its own sake by any political party or group in the country. It is disliked by many Labour backbenchers, who supported the Bill at the Second Reading only because they were persuaded that this course involved tactical advantages for their party. It is heartily disliked by the Conservative Party. It is supported by the Liberals only because they think it may be a stepping-stone towards the federal solution they have long advocated. It is supported by Scottish and Welsh nationalists because they regard it as a stepping-stone towards independence. The majority of the United Ulster Unionists are against it, seven opposing it on Second Reading while two supported it and one abstained.

Polls indicate that the Bill is generally welcomed by public opinion in Scotland, even though it has been criticised on various grounds. In Wales even this cannot be said. A poll sponsored by Harlech TV showed that 11 per cent of Welsh respondents were strongly in favour of the proposals, 16 per cent mildly in favour, 33 per cent neutral, 18 per cent mildly against, and 22 per cent strongly against (reported Harlech TV, 9 December 1976). It is therefore quite possible that Welsh electors would reject the proposals in the referendum that has been promised if the Bill is passed by Parliament. Public opinion in England has been deemed by the Government to be irrelevant, and English electors would not be permitted to vote in this referendum.

As a device for safeguarding Labour seats in Scotland at the next general election, the Bill has some merits. If it is passed, Labour will claim credit; if it is defeated, they will blame the Conservatives; and if it is passed by the Commons and defeated by the Lords, they will blame the latter. Some would say that Government leaders are thinking in terms of an even shorter time-span, the immediate advantage of the Bill being that it is likely to guarantee the support of nationalist MPs for the Government throughout 1977, a year in which Labour may lose its overall majority of one as a result of one or more by-election defeats. But in view of the sad history of British attempts to grapple with the issue of Home Rule for Ireland, one does not have to be a starry-eyed idealist to regret that British party leaders have not been able to adopt a more impartial and far-sighted approach to the problem of providing a measure of Home Rule for Scotland and Wales.

10

Conclusions and Speculations

There are two questions for discussion in this final chapter. One is the extent to which British political attitudes and practices may have to be modified to adapt the system so as to accommodate the growth of nationalist sentiments and movements. The second is the extent to which this development has been paralleled in other advanced countries and the reasons for the re-emergence of local loyalties and claims in this particular period of history.

The Need for a Change in British Attitudes
Whatever happens to the Scotland and Wales Bill, it seems clear that the United Kingdom is entering a new phase in its history, in which the centralised system of government that has served for the past two centuries will have to be modified. In the previous chapter reasons have been given for my view that the Scotland and Wales Bill is a thoroughly bad piece of legislation: misconceived, short-sighted and full of anomalies. If it is passed by Parliament it is more likely to prove a stepping-stone to further changes than to provide a stable system of government. But if the Bill does not get through Parliament this will not be the end of the matter, for the pressures of Scottish and Welsh nationalism will continue and other constitutional changes will be called for. It is not within the scope of this book to produce a blueprint for a new constitution. However, it is certainly appropriate to point out that one of the main obstacles to a successful process of adaptation to a changing situation is the deep reluctance of British political leaders and commentators to abandon certain long-standing assumptions about government that have now become outdated.

The first of these is the belief in parliamentary sovereignty. There has always been an element of myth in this doctrine, except perhaps for the years between the Reform Acts of 1832 and 1867. Before 1832 the power of Parliamentarians was limited by the Royal Prerogative and since 1867 it has been limited by the growing strength of party discipline. In the twentieth century

Parliament has surrendered all effective powers over finance and after the Second World War it surrendered most of its powers over defence. The defence of Britain now depends mainly on decisions made by the NATO Chiefs of Staff and the President of the United States. Britain's membership of the EEC has transferred law-making powers in many spheres from London to Brussels, and with that decision even the formal claim to sovereignty has been abandoned. There would consequently appear to be no good reason why this doctrine should be invoked in discussions of the transfer of legislative power to a Scottish Assembly.

Keen students of British political attitudes will not be surprised, however, to learn that the authors of the Kilbrandon Report do not see things in this light. They declare in their summary of recommendations that 'the sovereign powers of Parliament would be retained in full' and they assert in the body of the Report that: 'It is inherent in the concept of legislative devolution that Parliament would then, despite the transfer, retain in full its own power to legislate for the region on any matter' (Kilbrandon Report, pp. 478 and 232).

A second outdated belief is that the United Kingdom, alone among the world's democracies, does not need a written constitution. It has been convenient in the past to base our civil rights on the Common Law and our governmental practice on conventions that were understood and accepted by an establishment composed of gentlemen, it being assumed that men from outside this establishment who acquired social or political power could be socialised and co-opted into the magic circle. But it has been clear for some time that this legacy has lost much of its value.

The rights of immigrants and other minorities can no longer be covered adequately by the Common Law and in any case British citizens can now appeal to the European Court of Human Rights, which bases its judgements on a written declaration. The vast extension of government activities and institutions has created such a labyrinthine system, affecting the daily lives of all citizens, that there is now a good case for a written guide which will enable the man in the street to understand his own position and rights in relation to the bureaucracy. And the postwar period has seen the emergence of political actors who either do not understand or do not accept the established conventions.

A written constitution would of course require a special procedure for its amendment and a constitutional court for its interpretation. The Kilbrandon Report rejects such innovations, partly on the ground that they are new and partly because they would involve an extension of the role of the judiciary. It was said that the creation of a constitutional court with power to resolve disputes about governmental powers would be 'foreign to our own tradition of unitary government based upon the complete sovereignty of Parliament and upon the complete dissociation of the judiciary from matters of political policy' (Kilbrandon Report, p. 158). This is, of course, correct; but if a tradition has become obsolescent it is not much of an argument to say that changes would conflict with tradition. It is also relevant to note that in a situation of potential constitutional crisis the existence of a special process of constitutional amendment, requiring something more than a simple majority in Parliament, could well be a stabilising factor.

A third traditional attitude that could appropriately be modified is the mixture of complacency and scorn with which most British politicians regard federal systems of government. Reading between the lines, it may be surmised that the condemnation of the North American systems in the Kilbrandon Report owed something to the slowness of Canada and the United States in developing provisions for social security. But it is not necessary to go so far afield for models. Switzerland and West Germany combine federal systems with admirable social services; and since 1945 both countries have been governed more successfully than Britain, with higher rates of economic growth, less inflation, better industrial relations and (in the Swiss case) a highly developed set of conventions for accommodating linguistic and religious differences without conflict. It is impossible to think of any good reason why these systems of government should be regarded as less desirable than our own.

A federal solution for Britain has been advocated by the Liberal Party for many years and has recently been supported by the Moderator of the General Assembly of the Church of Scotland. It has had no support from either of the two main parties and, as noted above, it was condemned in rather sweeping terms by the Royal Commission on the Constitution. To adopt a federal constitution would of course be a complicated undertaking and would be a more radical reform than the British have ever previously made. But changes of one kind or another are imminent and the merits of federalism ought to be carefully weighed against the alternatives.

A federal solution would certainly have advantages over the lopsided arrangements proposed in the Scotland and Wales Bill, which would be unfair to the English and productive of endless conflicts over representation and finance. A federal solution would also be preferable to an outright rejection of the demands for Scottish and Welsh assemblies, which would involve the danger that large numbers of Scottish voters who favour devolution might turn their backs on the Westminster parties in disgust and vote for the SNP even though they did not actually want independence. If this were to happen the Union would face the possibility of disintegration because of inept political leadership rather than because of a conscious desire on the part of a majority of the Scottish people to sever their ties with the United Kingdom.

The fourth outdated belief which should be rooted out of our national consciousness is the smug conviction that our party system guarantees more effective government than the multiparty systems of most Continental democracies. Whenever the question of electoral reform is raised we are told by our leaders that the British system, though admittedly unfair, is demonstrably superior in its results because it provides a strong executive government with the power to take effective decisions. But it is now all too evident that our Continental neighbours have mostly done better than we have.

Our system enables a party in power to push whatever legislation it likes through the House of Commons, but power of that kind is not to be equated with strength and effectiveness. The alternating Labour and Conservative Governments since 1945 have failed to solve the country's economic problems, failed to control inflation and public expenditure, failed to improve industrial relations, failed to cope with the problems of Rhodesia, failed to control Commonwealth immigration to the extent that (according to the polls) 80 per cent of the British public desired, failed to enter the EEC at its inception (when Britain could have been a dominating influence within it), failed to solve the problems of Northern Ireland, and are failing to meet the challenge of Scottish and Welsh nationalism in an enlightened way.

By 1974 the British electorate was showing distinct signs of loss of confidence in the two main parties. Whereas 80 per cent of the electors had voted for one or other of the parties in the general election of 1951, only 54 per cent did so in October 1974. Many voted for the smaller parties and many simply abstained, Britain having dropped in this period from enjoying one of the highest turn-out records among Western democracies to having one of the lowest. Surveys of the extent to which electors identify with the main parties show that 'there has been, at least since 1964, a long-term trend for party identification in Britain to weaken' (Alt *et al.*, p. 290). There are reports that both main parties, particularly Labour, have suffered a serious drop in membership. And in January 1977 a Gallup Poll showed that, while 94 per cent of people thought the economic situation was serious, 74 per cent had 'little or no confidence' that our politicians could put it right (*The Scotsman*, 5 February 1977).

It is therefore at least arguable that the time has come to reform the electoral system so as to replace the system of 'adversary politics' between right and left by a system which would reflect more faithfully the varied (but not ideologically extreme) views of the electorate. This would lead to a situation in which coalition government was the norm, and the merits of this have recently been discussed in a volume of scholarly essays (see Finer). This is not the place to advocate any particular proposal for change, even if I were committed to one. My purpose is simply to suggest that electoral reform ought to have a place on the agenda, and that it will no longer do for our leaders to reiterate that the existing system has served us well.

Whether British politicians have the imagination to abandon these traditional assumptions seems, at the time of writing, to be very doubtful. The country may muddle through its current troubles and the United Kingdom may be preserved by the inherent loyalty of its citizens. But history will not forgive our leaders if they allow the kingdom to drift towards disintegration because they do not show themselves capable of considering the problems in a broader perspective than that provided by the party-political squabbles that have dominated Westminster politics since 1945.

An International Perspective

The growth of minority nationalist feelings is by no means confined to the United Kingdom. In Spain there are nationalist movements in the Basque country and Catalonia. In France the long-standing nationalist movements of Brittany and of the Basque country have recently been supplemented by agitations in Alsace, in Corsica and in Occitania. In Belgium the linguistic conflict between Flemish- and French-speaking groups shows no signs of abatement. In Canada the Quebec nationalist movement has grown markedly in strength and now commands a majority of seats in the Quebec legislative assembly.

In the United States the development of 'black nationalism' in the 1960s has been followed by an enhanced willingness on the part of Americans to accept the value of minority loyalties and cultures among other ethnic groups, so that the image of 'the melting pot' is being replaced by the image of a multi-ethnic society having some of the qualities of a mosaic. In the Soviet Union the rights of national minorities are still a bone of contention, and give rise to the same sort of problems as elsewhere. Thus, the 1958 reforms which enhanced the status of minority languages were simultaneously welcomed by enthusiasts for local cultures and resented by ambitious parents who preferred their children to be educated in Russian so as to enhance their prospects of a professional career. The conflict between communal interests and individual interests is the same in Uzbekistan as it is in Wales and it is true in both countries that (as Plaid Cymru leaders realise) the true nationalist cannot also be an individualist.

These developments belie the predictions that have been made by social scientists for more than a century. It is now clear that particularistic loyalties have not withered away as a consequence of the growth of industrial society and the impact of centralised government, although for a period they were so overshadowed by wider loyalties to the nation-state that they were inconspicuous and easily ignored.

In face of this situation some social scientists have devised a new theory, known as 'internal colonialism', which seeks to explain the recent manifestations of minority nationalism as the revolt of peripheral groups within the state who have been systematically exploited by the majority. But the evidence adduced to support this theory is patchy and inadequate. The relationship between the majority community and the minorities varies from one country to another and one period to another. It would be reasonable to describe Ireland's relationship to Britain in the eighteenth and nineteenth centuries as 'colonial' but unreasonable to describe Scotland's relationship to England in the twentieth century in this way. The trouble with this theory is that it is based on the unwarranted assumption that the dominant characteristic of modern society is economic exploitation, to which nationalist agitations (like almost any other agitation) are inevitable reactions. It is possible to view social trends through these spectacles but it is not necessary to do so, and I believe that the theory lacks the universal validity which its proponents claim for it. It is noticeable, for instance, that the Basque country and Catalonia are among the most prosperous areas of Spain, not the poorest.

My own view is that recent developments can be explained more clearly and less tendentiously in terms of two propositions. The first is that ethnic and local loyalties are enduring features of social life. No elaborate reasons are necessary to explain why people retain an attachment to their own ethnic group and the community in which they were brought up. These attachments may be overlaid by an acquired loyalty to a wider society and its political institutions, but the attachments remain and are likely to form the basis of political movements if the wider society loses some of its attractions.

The second proposition is that several recent developments have changed the balance of advantage between loyalty to the ethnic or local community and loyalty to the national society and state. There are three factors – all quite independent of one another – which have clearly changed this balance in the last two or three decades.

The first factor is the changed character of the international system. For the first time since the emergence of nation-states, the size of a country's population has ceased to bear a close relationship to its military security. The people of Belgium and Luxembourg are protected just as effectively by the NATO alliance and the American nuclear capacity as are the people of France and the United Kingdom. Size is also much less important than used to be the case in diplomatic disputes. The medium-sized states are so constrained by the web of international relationships that in some respects they have less freedom of manoeuvre than small states who for one reason or another find themselves in a favourable position, among which Iceland, Tanzania and Saudi Arabia are obvious examples. These changes in the international order have removed one of the main benefits to be derived from membership of a sizeable state.

The second factor is the development of supranational organisations like the EEC, the Council of Europe and the International Monetary Fund. Such organisations go some way towards giving citizens of small states the economic advantages that have hitherto been enjoyed only by citizens of large states. These include access to a larger market, the reduction of financial instability caused by local economic difficulties, and the opportunity for geographical mobility for members of the professional classes. The consequence of this development is that members of fairly small societies like Scotland can now gain many of the advantages of belonging to a large market for the exchange of goods and services without the sacrifice of local autonomy that has previously been a necessary concomitant. The rules of the EEC actually provide an incentive to disintegration, as an independent Scotland or Corsica would be entitled to its own representatives in Community institutions and would gain the important power of vetoing decisions in the Council of Ministers.

The third factor is the impact of television on cultural minorities, which is different in kind from the impact of other media. It is different because it brings the majority culture, often in its least attractive form, right into the living room. It is different because it captures the imagination and sympathies of children to a much greater extent than written material. A Welsh child who uses English at school but Welsh at home may retain a lifelong affection for the Welsh language, even though he has to use English at work. This is less likely to happen if he watches English television programmes each evening and adopts English and American film stars as his heroes, and such a transfer of allegiance may not be affected by the introduction of compulsory Welsh lessons at school.

Television also differs from the printed word in its enormous costs of production, so that minorities cannot support their own channels in the way that they support their own publishing firms. In view of these differences it is not surprising that the impact of television often provokes an angry reaction from the defenders of minority languages and cultures. People who would do nothing to prevent the gradual erosion of their language over the generations are stirred to protest if they see it threatened with extinction within their lifetime.

These developments do not of course create new nationalist movements out of thin air, for there has to be some feeling of national identity among the minority group to serve as a basis for them. But where sentiments exist, these developments create a climate in which minority nationalist movements may be expected to grow. Their growth in recent years has been assisted by two supplementary factors that should also be mentioned.

The first of these supplementary factors is the growth of political impatience. In an era when talk about the future is dominated by predictions of nuclear warfare, world famine and the exhaustion of energy resources, people are no longer willing to accept a situation which displeases them in the hope that things will be better for their children or grandchildren. There has never been a period in human history marked by the impatient demands that characterise the 1970s – for women's rights, gay rights, students' rights and prisoners' rights as well as for the rights of ethnic and national minorities.

The second supplementary factor is the development of television news programmes, which has proved to be of incalculable benefit to the propagandist activities of nationalist organisations. Whereas such movements in the past had to hold meetings and distribute pamphlets to reach a few thousand people, contemporary movements can command an audience of millions by any activity that attracts the television cameras. In 1976 the small and previously obscure South Moluccan nationalist movement, which wants Indonesia to grant independence to South Molucca, got an international television audience of tens (perhaps hundreds) of millions by the device of hijacking a suburban train in Holland. In Northern Ireland the impact of IRA demonstrations and bombing attacks has been immensely magnified by the extensive coverage given to them by television, to such an extent that the Secretary of State for Northern Ireland is reported to have told a meeting of top BBC officials 'that the IRA would have been defeated years ago had the Northern Ireland Office been allowed to direct BBC policy' (*Daily Mail*, 6 January 1977).

As both the three causal factors and the two supplementary factors are likely to be operative in the foreseeable future, it seems safe to predict that nationalistic movements will continue to proliferate and will make an increasing impact on the political scene. This means that the authority of the nation-state is likely to be further challenged, not only by the development of supranational institutions but also by claims for local autonomy which will in most cases be conciliated by the creation of sub-national institutions. Several European states have already moved some distance along this road, with federal systems in Switzerland, West Germany and Yugoslavia, a form of regionalism in Italy, and a complex system in Belgium designed to protect the interests of each linguistic group. The probability is that in the coming decades the nation-state, while continuing to exist, will increasingly be modified so as to fit in to a more complex system of decision making, in which citizens will be represented in and administered by four or five levels of government.

Bibliography

The following is not a bibliographical guide to the problems discussed, which would have to be very large, but is simply a list of the books and articles referred to in the text.

Abrams, Mark and Rose, Richard, *Must Labour Lose?* Harmondsworth: Penguin Books, 1960.
Ake, Claude, *A Theory of Political Integration.* Homewood, Illinois: The Dorsey Press, 1967.
Alt, James, Sarlvik, Bo. and Crewe, Ivor 'Partisanship and Policy Choice, Issue Preferences in the British Electorate, February 1974', *British Journal of Political Science*, vol. 6, 1976.
Barritt, Denis P. and Carter, Charles F., *The Northern Ireland Problem.* London: Oxford University Press, 1962; revised edition, 1972.
Beckett, J. C. (*a*), *A Short History of Ireland.* London: Hutchinson, 1952.
Beckett, J. C. (*b*), *The Making of Modern Ireland: 1603–1923.* London: Faber & Faber, 1966.
Bell, J. Bowyer, *The Secret Army: a History of the IRA. 1916–1970.* London: Sphere Books, 1972.
Bennett, Richard, *The Black and Tans.* London: New English Library, 1970.
Betts, Clive, *Culture in Crisis.* Upton, Merseyside: The Ffynnon Press, 1976.
Birch, A. H., *Federalism, Finance and Social Legislation.* Oxford: The Clarendon Press, 1955.
Boyce, D. G., *Englishmen and Irish Troubles.* London: Jonathan Cape, 1972.
Brown, A. J., *The Framework of Regional Economics in the United Kingdom.* Cambridge University Press, 1972.
Cameron Report, *Disturbances in Northern Ireland.* Belfast: HMSO, Cmd 532 of 1969.
Carter, H. and Thomas, J. G., 'The Referendum on the Sunday Opening of Licensed Premises in Wales as a Criterion of a Culture Region', *Regional Studies*, vol. 3, 1969.
Chapman, Brian, *British Government Observed.* London: George Allen & Unwin, 1963.
Commission on the Constitution:
Research Paper 1: *Federalism and Decentralisation in the Federal Republic of Germany.* London: HMSO, 1973.
Research Paper 7: *Devolution and Other Aspects of Government: An Attitudes Survey.* London: HMSO, 1973.
Research Paper 10: *Financial and Economic Aspects of Regionalism and Separatism.* London: HMSO, 1973.
See also Royal Commission on the Constitution.
Commission on the Restoration of the Irish Language, *Summary, in English, of Final Report.* Dublin: Stationery Office, 1963.
Daniel, J. E., *Welsh Nationalism: What It Stands For.* London: Foyles Welsh Co., 1937.

Dennis, Jack, Lindberg, Leon and McCrone, Donald, 'Support for Nation and Government among English Children', *British Journal of Political Science*, vol. I, 1971.

Devolution to Scotland and Wales: Supplementary Statement. London: HMSO, Cmnd 6585 of 1976.

Edwards, Owen Dudley, Evans, Gwynfor, Rhys, Ioan and MacDiarmid, Hugh, *Celtic Nationalism*. London: Routledge & Kegan Paul, 1968.

Evans, Gwynfor *(a)*, *Wales Can Win*. Llandybie, Carmarthenshire: Christopher Davies, 1973.

Evans, Gwynfor *(b)*, *Nonviolent Nationalism*. New Maldon, Surrey: The Fellowship of Reconciliation, 1973.

Evans, Gwynfor *(c)*, *A National Future for Wales*. Cardiff: Plaid Cymru, 1975.

Finer, S. E. (ed.), *Adversary Politics and Electoral Reform*. London: Anthony Wigram, 1975.

Fishman, J. A., *Language in Sociocultural Change*. Stanford University Press, 1972.

Fisk, Robert, *The Point of No Return*. London: André Deutsch, 1975.

Fitzgibbon, Constantine, *Red Hand: the Ulster Colony*. London: Michael Joseph, 1971.

Fowler, H. W., *A Dictionary of Modern English Usage*. London: Oxford University Press, 1926; rev. edn 1937.

Freight Transport Statistics. The statistics for freight transport within Britain were calculated by the author from data supplied by the British Railways Board. The Irish figures were taken from the *Irish Statistical Bulletin* and the *Digest of Port Statistics*.

Ghai, Dharam, 'Territorial Distribution of the Benefits and Costs of the East African Common Market', in Colin Leys and Peter Robson (eds), *Federation in East Africa: Opportunities and Problems*. Nairobi: Oxford University Press, 1965.

Giglioli, P. (ed.), *Language and Social Context*. Harmondsworth: Penguin Books, 1972.

Gittins Report, *Primary Education in Wales*. London: Department of Education and Science, 1968. (Report by a committee of the Central Advisory Council on Education.)

Gonzales-Casanova, Pablo, 'Internal Colonialism and National Development', *Studies in Comparative International Development*, vol. 1, 1965.

Griffith, Gwilym O., *The New Wales*. Liverpool: Hugh Evans & Sons, 1913.

Hanham, H. J. *Scottish Nationalism*. London: Faber & Faber, 1969.

Harbinson, J. F., *The Ulster Unionist Party, 1882–1973*. Belfast: Blackstaff Press, 1973.

Harris, Rosemary, *Prejudice and Tolerance in Ulster*. Manchester University Press, 1972.

Hechter, Michael, *Internal Colonialism: The Celtic Fringe in British National Development, 1536–1966*. London: Routledge & Kegan Paul, 1975.

Holt, Edgar, *Protest in Arms*. London: Putnam, 1960.

Hughes-Parry Report, *Legal Status of the Welsh Language*. London: HMSO, Cmnd 2785 of 1965.

Jaensch, Dean, 'The Scottish Vote 1974: a Re-aligning Party System?' *Political Studies*, vol. XXIV, 1976.

Jahoda, Gustav, 'The Development of Children's Ideas about Country and Nationality', *The British Journal of Educational Psychology*, vol. XXXIII, 1963.

Jones, Alun R. and Thomas, Gwyn, *Presenting Saunders Lewis*. Cardiff: University of Wales Press, 1973.

Jones, R. Tudor, *The Desire of Nations*. Llandybie, Dyfed: Christopher Davies, 1974.

Kariel, Henry S., 'Creating Political Reality', *American Political Science Review*, vol. LXIV, 1970.

Kee, Robert, *The Green Flag*. London: Weidenfeld & Nicolson, 1972.

Kellas, James G., *The Scottish Political System*. Cambridge University Press, 1973.

Kermack, W. R., *The Scottish Highlands: a Short History*. Edinburgh: Johnson & Bacon, 1957.

Kilbrandon Report, see Royal Commission on the Constitution.

Koestler, Arthur, *The Heel of Achilles*. London: Hutchinson, 1974; Picador Edition by Pan Books, 1976.

Lewis, Robyn, *Second-Class Citizen*. Gwasg Gomer, Llandysul: J. D. Lewis & Sons, 1969.

Lewis, Saunders, *Principles of Nationalism*. First published 1926 in Welsh, reprinted in a bilingual edition by Plaid Cymru, Cardiff, 1975.

Lockwood, W. B. *Languages of the British Isles Past and Present*. London: André Deutsch, 1975.

Lyons, F. S. L., *Ireland since the Famine*. London: Weidenfeld & Nicolson, 1971; revised edition: Fontant, 1973.

McCrone, Gavin, *Scotland's Future: The Economics of Nationalism*. Oxford: Basil Blackwell, 1969.

Mackintosh, J. P., *The British Cabinet*, London: Stevens & Sons, 1962.

Macmillan, Harold, *The Blast of War: 1939–1945*. London: Macmillan, 1967.

Macnamara, J., *Bilingualism and Primary Education*. Edinburgh University Press, 1966.

McNeill, Ronald, *Ulster's Stand for Union*. London: John Murray, 1922.

Madgwick, P. J. (a), *The Politics of Rural Wales*. London: Hutchinson, 1973.

Madgwick, P. J. (b), 'Linguistic Conflict in Wales', in Glyn Williams (ed.), *Social and Cultural Changes in Contemporary Wales*. London: Routledge & Kegan Paul, 1977.

Mansergh, Nicholas, *The Irish Question, 1840–1921*. London: George Allen & Unwin, 3rd edn, 1975.

May, R. J., *Federalism and Fiscal Adjustment*. Oxford: The Clarendon Press, 1969.

Memorandum of Dissent, see Royal Commission on the Constitution.

Morgan, Kenneth O., *Wales in British Politics 1868–1932*. Cardiff: University of Wales Press, 1970.

O'Hagan, J. W., *The Economy of Ireland: Policy and Performance*. Dublin: Irish Management Institute, 1975.

O Cuiv, Brian, *A View of the Irish Language*. Dublin: Stationery Office, 1969.

O'Hegarty, P. S., *Victory of Sinn Fein*. Dublin: Talbot Press, 1924.

O'Neill, Terence, *Ulster at the Crossroads*. London: Faber & Faber, 1969.

Paor, Liam de, *Divided Ulster*. Harmondsworth: Pelican Books, 1970.

Philip, Alan Butt, *The Welsh Question*. Cardiff: University of Wales Press, 1975.

Pride, J. and Holmes, J. (eds), *Sociolinguistics*. Harmondsworth: Penguin Books, 1972.

Pringle, M. L. Kellmer, 'Regional Differences in the Behaviour and

Adjustment of 7-year olds: Some Results from the National Child Development Study', a paper read at the 1969 meeting of the British Association for the Advancement of Science.

Rees, William, *The Union of England and Wales*. Cardiff: University of Wales Press, 1967.

Riddell, Patrick, *Fire over Ulster*. London: Hamish Hamilton, 1970.

Road Transport Survey, see *Survey of the Transport of Goods by Road, 1967–1968*. London: HMSO, 1969.

Rose, Richard (a), *Governing without Consensus*. London: Faber & Faber, 1971.

Rose, Richard (b), *Northern Ireland: Time of Choice*. Washington, DC: American Enterprise Institute for Public Policy Research, 1976.

Royal Commission on the Constitution:
  Report. London: HMSO, Cmnd 5460 of 1973.
  Memorandum of Dissent. London: HMSO, Cmnd 5460–1 of 1973.
  Written Evidence, vols. 1–9. London: HMSO, 1973.
  Minutes of Evidence, vols. I–V. London: HMSO, 1973.

Smout, T. C., *A History of the Scottish People: 1560–1830*. London: Collins, 1969.

Spender, J. A. and Asquith, Cyril, *Life of Lord Oxford and Asquith*. London: Hutchinson, 1932.

Stavenhagen, Rodolpho, 'Classes, Colonialism, and Acculturation', *Studies in Comparative International Development*, vol. 1, 1965.

Stewart, A. T. Q., *The Ulster Crisis*. London: Faber & Faber, 1967.

Thomas, Ned, *The Welsh Extremist*. Talybont, Cardiganshire: Y Lolfa, 1973.

Trevelyan, G. M., *English Social History*. London: Longmans, Green & Co., 3rd edn, 1946.

Wall, Maureen, 'Partition: the Ulster Question', in T. Desmond Williams (ed.), *The Irish Struggle: 1916–1926*. London: Routledge & Kegan Paul, 1966.

Williams, David, *A History of Modern Wales*. London: John Murray, 1951.

Williams, T. Desmond (ed.), *The Irish Struggle, 1916–1926*. London: Routledge & Kegan Paul, 1966.

Woodburn, J. B., *The Ulster Scot*. London: H. R. Allenson, 1914.

Woodham-Smith, Cecil, *The Great Hunger*. London: Hamish Hamilton, 1962.

Index

DI